THE FLABBERGAST FARM FIGHTS BACK

E.J. DAUBERT

ISBN-13: 979-8-9888134-0-8

Library of Congress Control Number: 2023915380

Published by E.J. Daubert,

Hogsmill Press, Springfield, VA 22153

First printed in 2023 in the USA

Cover illustration by GetCovers.com

For Scott

CHAPTER ONE

Welcome to the Flabbergast Farm!

"Morning, Mr. Mailman."

The mailman paused as he reached into the red bag slung over one shoulder. He leaned over the gate and surveyed the empty farmyard. An Old English Sheepdog squatted on the path behind the fence, head cocked to one side.

"Wondered if you had any treats on you. Maybe in your bag? Hiding in a pocket?" said the voice.

"Treats?" The mailman frowned, shoving the bill of his cap higher as he scratched his head. He peered around the edges of the hedge.

"A Good Boy biscuit. Or a Meaty Treat. If you've got one."

The dog sat a few feet away from him, mouth open and tongue hanging out. Sparkling green eyes peeked out from under a mop of shaggy gray and white fur, spattered at the ends with dried mud. It looked as if the dog was grinning.

The mailman patted his pockets for a dog biscuit, then realized what a silly boy he was.

"Molly," he said, a smile spreading slowly on his face. "Is that you, Molly? You having me on again? Doing one of your tricks? Come on out, girl."

The dog whined and slumped to the ground. "Never mind. Just a biscuit. Don't worry if it's too much effort. I wouldn't want to be a bother." He stuck his nose between his paws and squeezed his eyes shut.

"Oh, Winston." The mailman patted his pockets again and this time found half a dog biscuit shoved at the bottom. He drew it out and held up the stale treat. "Here we are, buddy. Don't look so upset." He looked around again, as if searching for someone, then raised his voice. "Molly! Great trick. Where are you hiding?"

A blur of movement skidded around the corner of the house, up the path and slid to a halt behind the pile of sheepdog.

"Oh, there you are." The mailman wagged his finger at her. "You really had me going there, Molly. I thought for a minute you've got a talking dog."

The girl bent double, gasping for breath, but she tried to laugh along. She flapped one hand and shook her head, but there was no air in her lungs for proper words. "No, not..." *No, not again*, she thought.

The mailman snorted. "Of course not, silly, who would believe you had a talking dog. I mean - what next? A singing goat?"

"Pigs, actually."

Molly threw herself on top of Winston, wrapping her arms around his head. *Winston!* The mailman beamed at her and waggled his finger again.

"You lot should be on the telly," he said. "Oh wait, you are!" He guffawed at the punch line, tried to pat his strained waistcoat with full hands and nearly dropped the stack of mail from one hand and the dog biscuit from the other. "You know, it's quite amazing what you and your grandmother have done here, Molly. A whole farm crammed into one back garden - the rest of this street think they're pushing the boat out with a new flower bed. Chestnut Crescent wasn't such an exciting street when I started this round.

Anyway, must get on. Number 6 has her new garden ornaments catalog she's been looking forward to. And number 2 has a lovely postcard from his nephew in Australia. So, here you are, Molly, make sure your grandma gets these. One day, you must tell me how you manage all these tricks. Last time I saw a ventriloquist that good was at the seaside when I was a kiddie."

Molly grabbed the pile of slithery brown envelopes, catalogs and leaflets from him and nodded. "Thanks, I'll take them straight in."

"Totally different voice too," said the mailman.

"Amazing, Molly. Here you go, Winston." He held the treat over the gate. The dog's ears pricked up. In one easy bound, Winston leaped up and grabbed the biscuit between his teeth. He knocked the mail from Molly's hands and the pieces scattered everywhere.

"-Ank 'oo!" said the dog, galloping away across the yard before Molly could get her hands on him again.

That dog! she thought.

The mailman shook his head and laughed. "Brilliant! Absolutely brilliant!" He was still chuckling as he headed to the next house.

***

Molly gathered up the fallen envelopes. Winston had disappeared.

"Winston!" she called after the dog. "Oh, what will we do with you?" But it was no use, he wouldn't have listened anyway. Winston was always in the middle of any chaos in the farmyard. *He's up to my waist,* Molly thought. *But he still thinks he's an adorable little puppy. Nothing is ever his fault.*

On a normal farm, an Old English sheepdog would have to herd sheep. Luckily, Winston had found his way to their farm. He wouldn't have lasted two minutes anywhere else. Winston was a hopeless herder. The sheep always laughed at his antics and scooted in the other direction. At least here he could put his special talent to good use.

All the animals living at the Flabbergast Farm were performing animals. Instead of producing eggs and milk for sale, they sang for their supper. Or danced. Sometimes, the job required barking at people about inattentive children who had fallen down a well. One TV advert had involved three chickens, a singing pig and a donkey doing a tap dance. The Flabbergast Farm was famous for having the best trained animals in the business, although nobody outside the farm knew how they managed it.

Molly shuffled the mail into a more manageable pile and set off through the farmyard. Winston's trail of destruction was easy to follow - a trampled flower bed here, a knocked-over pail of feed there. He had barreled through the pig pen. The pigs had been playing Scrabble, and Winston had left a scattering of yellow tiles and two snorting Gloucester Old Spots in his wake.

Molly paused. Hands on her hips, she plonked both feet firmly on the path and looked around the Flabbergast Farm. *I suppose it is quite unusual* she thought. *If you're not expecting it.* The three-bedroom, detached house looked the same as all the others on the street. From the front gate. But behind the house stood an assortment of animal shelters.

The duckpond along the left side of the garden led to a rickety stable which leaned against the fence in the corner. Next to that, a cow shed, then the chicken coop. There was the neatest pig pen you have ever seen slap bang in the middle of the farmyard, then the sheep paddock and a shed to the right for the llama and goat type residents. Vegetable patches and flowerbeds squeezed in wherever they could, but this back garden was definitely about animals.

Molly scanned the farmyard again, this time for any dog size movement. There was no sign of him. But she heard a strange whirring noise from behind her, and twisted to see what it was.

A half-crazed chicken zoomed between Molly's legs, knocking her into the biggest, wettest, muddiest puddle in the yard. Molly looked up and watched the chicken's wobbly path as it pin balled between four horse hooves, over the back of a pig and across a puddle. Mud flew. Feathers ruffled. The chicken flapped her way through the farmyard, straight up the rickety ladder into the chicken house.

"Bella," Molly yelled. "Are you alright?"

An upset chicken was the last thing Molly needed today. From the state of the weather to the color of her eggs, Bella always worried about something. But she normally just pecked the ground and flapped her wings about it.

"Can I help?" shouted Molly. She struggled up from the slimy ground, wiping her hands on her oversized tee-shirt. The mail was a lost cause; wet, covered in brown sludge, and torn in places. Her grandmother would not be amused about that. She crammed the bills into the back pocket of her jeans and left the rest of the pile with the unhappy pigs.

"Bella - what's wrong?" Molly shouted towards

the chicken coop. She counted off the possibilities on her fingers.

"OK, Bella. You had - one - a perfect white egg this morning," she muttered. "Two - you've not lost any feathers. Three - you've got plenty of feed in the bowl. I know the weather is miserable, but that shouldn't set you racing round the yard like that, unless it's to keep warm. This must be something to do with Winston."

There was no answer from the chicken in her coop. Molly had no choice but to go in after her.

CHAPTER TWO

Chicken Drama

Molly slopped along the rest of the muddy path towards the chicken coop, leaving a sticky trail of boot prints behind her. The two chutney brown braids framing her face were already unraveling slightly as they swung back and forth to match her stride. Molly brushed her hair out of her eyes, leaving a smudge of brown muck across her forehead, and took one last look around for the lost sheepdog.

Oh well. He'll turn up when he's hungry. Molly shoved her hands into the pockets of her jeans to warm them up and carried on up the path to talk to Bella.

The chicken coop lurked near the house. It looked like a beaten up, cobbled together wooden shack. On the outside. The blue paint peeled from the wooden frame and the door hung crookedly from its hinges. The weathered shingles on the roof were roughly torn at the edges, but they held every downpour out. The chickens inside stayed cozy and dry even during heavy thunderstorms. Molly made sure of that.

Taking care of the coop had been one of her first jobs when she came to live at the farmyard, perfectly sized to crawl inside and make repairs. She spent hours fixing loose shingles, filling gaps and prettying it up. Making comfy cushions to line the nest boxes. Flowered curtains for the tiny windows. Inside, it was the fanciest of chicken hotels. The chickens adored "our Molly" and liked to chat and cluck with her about all sorts of things, from the variations in egg size and color to the quality of feed these days. They loved to hear her stories about school- the crazy teachers who wrote on the wall, children being sent outside to run around like baby chicks, and best of all, the excitement of lunch breaks.

Now Molly had reached the heady heights of four feet and ten inches, crawling inside tested her flexibility. Only her head and shoulders fitted through the door comfortably. Molly knelt down and squeezed in as far as she could. Bella huddled on the blue nest at the far end of the coop. The chicken stuck her beak up in the air and turned away at the sight of Molly.

"Oh Bella," said Molly. "Are you OK?" Bella sniffed the sniff of an offended chicken and turned her beak even further. "Was it Winston? That dog knows he's not supposed to chase you."

"Winston tore my new sweater!" cried the

chicken. "My new blue one you made me for my birthday! I haven't even worn it yet. I was about to take off this one and put my lovely new blue one on when he grabbed it and slobbered on it and ripped it away from me. That dog is a menace!" She pecked at the bright pink wool sweater.

"This old, pink one is nowhere near as nice. It's covered in mud and grass now, there's a huge hole in it, and I want my new blue one back!" Her wail ended in a sob. The tears broke free and ran down the chicken's beak.

"OK, OK, calm down," said Molly. Something noisy, messy or smelly happened all the time in the farmyard. *Why today though? I really don't have time for chicken drama,* she thought.

"I'll go and find Winston and get it back for you. I'll be able to mend it, I'm sure." Molly backed out of the chicken house and surveyed the farmyard. She wrapped her arms around herself and shivered in the chill of the late September morning.

***

A sense of peace settled over the farmyard. The pigs snuffled around in their pen, gossiping about the thrilling chicken chase and cleaning each other of mud splatters. Next to the pig pen stood a paddock crammed with a horse, cows, goats, a donkey and a llama, but distinctly empty of Old English sheepdog.

Molly frowned as her gaze traveled over the rest of the farmyard. The flock of geese happily milled about. They pecked at the ground and splashed in the sludge at the edge of the duck pond. Some of the chickens followed Robbie the Rooster as if he were a rock star; others scratched at their new pile of music magazines.

The doors to all the sheds were shut. The stable in the corner looked silent and empty. The familiar smell of warm manure oozed from that corner of the farmyard. Even the breeze which had whipped Molly's cheeks to pinkness earlier had settled down to a chilly whisper.

Where can you be, Winston? Molly absentmindedly tugged on one of her braids, which had practically escaped from its elastic band. *And what have you done with that sweater?* Chicken sweaters were not easy things to knit, especially if you were twelve years old and didn't have much spare time or natural talent for knitting. It had taken Molly weeks to finish, and Winston had ruined it in minutes.

Molly Pickering may not have been a natural knitter, but she had plenty of other talents. Moving to her grandmother's farm at the tender age of five had given her a chance to discover some unusual abilities. Slightly unexpected ones for a suburban schoolgirl anyway. Chestnut Crescent was smack dab in the middle of Suburbiton, a small town hidden away in the outskirts of The Big City. The Flabbergast Farm was not what you would normally expect to find in the back yard in an English suburb.

By her sixth birthday, Molly could milk a cow.

By the age of seven, she was in charge of the goats too, even with their frisky sense of humor. Horse grooming and riding were part of Molly's daily routine from the time she could walk and climb a step ladder; and no one could coax a stubborn chicken to lay an egg like Molly could. Not that it helped much at school, but all the important stuff happened at the farmyard anyway.

***

Molly tapped her foot. *Could a dog that big hide in the water barrel or the compost bin? Perhaps he's in the stables after all?* She swiveled in that direction, but a self-satisfied purr in her ear stopped Molly in her tracks.

"Winston's under the truck," said a voice as smooth as melting butter. "He thinks we won't find him if he keeps his paws over his eyes. That dog is so stupid."

"Freya! That is not a nice thing to say." *Even if it's sometimes a bit true.* Winston often did things that made you wonder where he'd left his brain that morning. "And you shouldn't be a tattletale," she scolded the smug black cat.

"I saw what he did to Bella's sweater. He should leave her alone. That dog is too much."

"Winston doesn't mean it. He gets carried away."

"Just like a dog. Cats never get carried away. We're always in control of ourselves. That dog doesn't care if he upsets anyone else. He wants to run around and make as much noise as possible. If only he'd do it somewhere else, with the volume turned down preferably."

"Freya, you say such mean things. You'd miss Winston if he left us."

"I doubt it. It would at least be quieter. That dog never knows how to keep his mouth shut. He started trying to talk to the newspaper boy this morning. Can you imagine?"

"I can," said Molly. "Did he notice?"

"Winston wanted to know if the boy had a spare dog biscuit. He tried the usual woof, woof, beg routine, and when that didn't work, the stupid dog asked straight out."

"No! Not again?"

"Oh yes. Please sir…"

Molly hardly dared to ask what happened next. She stared at Freya. Is *the farm's secret already out? Does everyone in the world know about our talking animals?* The pause dragged on.

"And?" asked Molly. "What happened?" She could hear the begging tone in her own voice.

"Luckily, your grandmother happened to open the front door to see if the newspaper had arrived. The boy must have thought he heard an old lady asking. I mean, he's not daft enough to think it would be the dog, is he?"

"He didn't realize?"

"No. Came close though. He gave your grandma a really funny look when he handed over the Suburbiton Observer."

Molly sagged against the Jeep. *So the mailman wasn't the first person that Winston had nearly let the cat out of the bag to. Even this morning. That dog!*

"I'll talk to him about it. Again. Winston knows better than that."

"We know what would happen. It would be the end of the performing tricks and the start of people pointing and worrying. No more TV studios. We'd all be shipped off to zoos or laboratories before you could say "dog biscuits." You know it, I know it, everybody knows it. Even that dog, but he doesn't ever think first. You need to get it into his thick head, Molly. Before he ruins it for all of us."

"I know, I know. I will, Freya. But you'll have to keep an eye on Winston whenever I have to go to school. I'll figure something out, but I need time. And we don't have time today."

Freya merely shrugged one shoulder, stretched both her hind legs out behind her, yawned slowly and leaped down lightly from the top of the battered blue truck. Freya had scored a small victory against that ridiculous dog. She silently disappeared up the garden path, her tail upright and paws crossing delicately in an elegant exit.

Molly avoided that feud, but Winston managed to get himself in trouble frequently. *I'll have to talk to him about it. And, of course, retrieve the chicken sweater and see what could be done about that. I'll deal with the dog first.*

Molly bent over the front of the truck and peered into the gloom underneath. She squinted at a vague lump in the middle of the blackness, but the smell of damp carpet gave him away.

"Winston," she murmured. "Winston...." The gray lump shuffled and two green orbs glowed back at her. "C'mon, Winston. Come out. Bring the chicken sweater. Bella's upset right now, but she'll get over it. Come on out, fella. We don't have time for all this."

He answered with a low growl.

"Winston, you silly billy. I bet if you take Bella back her sweater, once I've mended it of course, and a nice handful of potato peelings, then she'll forgive you for getting over enthusiastic about her sweater."

"Bella hates me," said Winston in a low voice. "Everybody hates me. Especially the cat. I'll stay under here until everybody goes away." He sighed deeply and buried his nose in his paws.

"Nobody hates you, Winston. Bella will calm down, and Freya - well - she worries about keeping everyone safe. Freya thinks she's smarter than everybody else, and she doesn't always stop to think how unkind she sounds. Why don't you come out?"

Molly reached a hand under the truck and tried to pat the ball of fluffiness. Winston reluctantly began to edge towards her, head low to the ground, one paw after the other. He paused before his head popped out from under the truck. His leathery nose tipped up and Winston sniffed the air, as if reading it. Somehow, Winston always knew something was about to happen a brief second before it started.

The front doorbell rang distantly inside the

house. The ringing also set off a series of flashing red lights, which spun like sirens and gave the gloomy gray sky a spooky glow. Time for all hands on deck when that happened.

Molly jumped into action. Skidded across the yard to the paddock. Grabbed the purple feather boa from around the llama's long bushy neck. Dived into the pig pen. Hid the game of Scrabble the pigs had left out. Shoved everything into an empty barrel. Her long limbs cleared the pig pen fence like an Olympic hurdler and she sprinted twice around the pen herding the squawking chickens into the middle of the yard.

Molly dashed back to the pen. Threw a grubby old tarpaulin over the pile of magazines the animals had been inspecting. Darted about closing locks and sliding bolts on doors and gates. *As if we really keep the animals in their pens.*

Between the time the doorbell rang and her grandmother opened the front door, exactly one minute and thirty-seven seconds had passed. They had practiced countless times over the years, but they finished with only seconds to spare. The front gate creaked open sharply. Footsteps clattered along the path. A face peered into the farmyard. *He's getting quicker each time. One day he'll catch us with something out of place, and then the jig will be up.*

But, thought Molly as she looked around the farmyard, *not today*. It really did look normal this time. Good job, considering who had walked into the farmyard.

CHAPTER THREE

The Arrival of the Bowler Hat

Mr. Bennet looked as if he had never seen a farmyard before. Despite the addition of a rather smart pair of green wellington boots to his outfit, he appeared to be in the wrong place. Perhaps it was the smart black suit with the tiny pinstripes. Possibly the shiny leather briefcase he carried everywhere he went.

But Molly thought it was mostly the hat.

Mr. Bennet wore a spotlessly clean, round, black bowler hat at all times. The type of hat that traditionally sits on the head of a very boring British middle-aged man. *Him and that hat. He wears it even in the middle of summer. It makes him look like he goes off to work every morning at a fancy bank, festooned with pillars and cherubs and a liveried doorman.*

In her mind, Molly dropped a low curtsy, her skirts brushing the ground and her eyelids modestly lowered. *It's what the hat would like. I wonder if it's disappointed that Mr. Bennet is just a lowly Government Inspector of Farms and Livestock. I bet it watches him at dinner with a slightly disapproving air and he brushes it clean every night before bed. If only Mr. Bennet had a real pet of his own. Perhaps then his life wouldn't be ruled by the bowler hat.*

Molly could always tell what sort of mood Mr. Bennet arrived in, simply by the state of his hat. Some days he appeared with the brim jammed down past the tips of his ears. Those days the visit would be brief and angry. He'd usually already had a full day of sputtering at other people and putting big X's on his paperwork. He'd examine everything in minute detail on those days, looking for any reason to cancel the farm's license and put a violent red mark at the bottom of the page.

On that type of day, Molly resorted to some inventive distractions. Like a hive full of bees mysteriously getting loose, a cow taking a distinct liking to the clipboard, or a highly unexpected and extremely localized shower of rain right by the kitchen door.

Mind you, on other days, Mr. Bennet arrived with the well brushed bowler perched rakishly over one eye, twinkling with excitement at the idea of catching them out. He would bounce across the farmyard with enthusiasm, as if they were all playing a fun game of 'Guess the missing regulation'. On one notable occasion, the inspector had turned up with his hat sitting back on his head at a rather jaunty angle. It gave Molly and her grandmother great hopes of an easy inspection. But it turned out later that the wind had blown it there as he got off the bus.

On this occasion, Mr. Bennet slid past the length of the mud splattered horse trailer on the driveway and appeared at the edge of the farmyard. The green wellington boots stepped over a large muddy puddle and guided him to a small patch of grass, where Mr. Bennet slowly surveyed the farmyard with a disdainful stare. His perfectly symmetrical mustache twitched as he took in every detail around him.

Molly slid to a halt in front of the inspector. "Mr. Bennet," she said, trying to catch her breath. "It's so lovely to see you again. Did you have anything in particular you wanted to see today? We've got cows, and sheep and chickens. Perhaps a goat?" Molly caught sight of the goat cantering across the yard in their direction and immediately changed her mind about that. "Actually, no goat. You don't need a goat on a morning like this. What would you like to see?'

The bowler hat had sunk so far it rested on the inspector's eyebrows. *Not a good sign.* Mr. Bennet's nose rose an inch or so.

"I require access to the entire farm, as per The Government Act of 1893 pertaining to the Inspection of Farmyard and Animal Husbandry Premises." He sniffed. "As I always do."

"Last time I paid this farm visit, you managed to" - Mr. Bennet peered down his nose, as if he didn't believe the words coming from his own mouth - "satisfy the conditions of the Animals in Television Licensing Act of 1964. Well, today I will be investigating the conditions in which your livestock reside."

Molly tried to keep up with all his long words. *Last time was about the TV performance license*, she thought. *This time he wants to check the animals' beds.* The inspector wagged a finger at Molly.

"Today you won't fob me off with cow chases or emergency trips to the vet, or any of your other tricks. Today I will see it all!" He rested his shiny black briefcase on top of the feed bin, snipped open the two locks, and out came the clipboard and the clicky pen. Mr. Bennet meant business. He shut the briefcase again, neatly and precisely, and clasped the clipboard to his chest. "Now, I wish to start at...." He peered down at the top of his list and jabbed it with the clicky pen. "Ah yes, the chickens."

The kitchen door slammed open against the wall. Mr. Bennet jumped several inches. His clicky pen flew up into the air, flipping and twisting in somersaults, then arcing downwards towards a muddy puddle. Molly gasped and reached for it as it fell, but too late. Winston got there first, snatching the pen out of the air and sliding through the slick mud to land at Mr. Bennet's feet, spraying sludge everywhere.

He offered the spit covered pen to the Inspector. Mr. Bennet gingerly removed it from the dog's teeth with the tips of his fingers, trying to touch the pen as little as possible. Out came a perfectly pressed white handkerchief to wipe the slime from his favorite pen and the specks of mud from his chin.

"Thank you," he said, his tone chilly.

"Grandma!" said Molly, with relief in her voice, as her grandmother appeared at the kitchen entrance. No one could make an entrance like her grandma. She stood in the doorway, back straight and chin up, prepared to take on the world. A ray of weak sunlight broke through the grumbling clouds and danced across her softly lined face. Molly beamed at her.

The old lady saw Mr. Bennet and his lemon sucking expression. She took note of the bowler hat sitting low over his eyebrows.

Grandma inhaled a deep breath, smoothed her frizzled white hair back and pushed up her baggy cardigan sleeves. Setting her lips in a tight smile, she scurried over to join them, with the chickens clucking madly behind her in a line.

"Mr. Bennet, how wonderful to see you again. It must have been at least three weeks since your last visit. Is there anything in particular you would like to see today? I can put the kettle on if you're staying. I've baked a particularly delicious celery and treacle tart." Grandma winked at Molly. Mr. Bennet had never been known to accept as much as a crumb of her inventive pastries, but it was worth a try.

"I wish to see the farmyard, the whole farmyard. I know there's something you're not telling me," said Mr. Bennet. "Every single inch of it." The animals shuffled obediently into a sort of line, ready for inspection.

Now Mr. Bennet may not have been a kind man nor an imaginative one, but neither was he stupid. The inspector knew that something unusual went on at The Flabbergast Farm, but he could not, despite repeated visits, work out what it was.

There is something which drives a man like Mr. Bennet and that is the need to have all the boxes on his clipboard neatly ticked by the end of the day. But that never seemed to happen when he visited this farmyard. Mr. Bennet's eyebrows arched together as he tried for the hundred and tenth time to work out what was going on right under his nose. Finally, he thought he had it.

"How do they know when you want them to line up?" he said, prodding his clicky pen at Molly triumphantly. "It's not natural for animals to be so well behaved."

Uh oh, thought Molly.

"Well, they are trained animals, Mr. Bennet," her grandma interrupted. "How could they perform on acting jobs if they weren't? It would be chaos. They're all trained to line up and stand still when someone is taking a good look at them."

The animals all tried to look as if they weren't listening to this exchange. Molly saw a hoof tapping, several chickens rolling their eyes, and

Daisy the cow began to whistle tunelessly. Molly put her finger to her lips as she stood behind the pinstriped inquisitor and glared at the culprits. They all froze in position. She could still see a couple of grins trying to break through. Molly glared harder at them.

Mr. Bennet tapped his finger against his mustache thoughtfully. Something else bothered him.

"The hats. Why are the sheep wearing hats?" he asked at last. "That is not a normal thing for sheep to do."

He's right. They're still wearing their blue berets.

The sheep were so attached to their favorite hats, they refused to give them up. Donald the donkey snorted at the thought of his special straw hat hidden away unnecessarily in the stable stall. The sheep herded themselves into a corner and nodded away under their floppy felt berets. Fetching though they were, they did not help the animals look normal.

"Baa...Baa..." said the first one, and then nudged the one next to her to join in.

"Baaaaaa... Um... Baaaaaa," said the next sheep in line.

The third beret bearer rolled her eyes, then turned and whispered something in the second one's ear. The second beret bobbed up and down in response. They both opened their mouths wide, ready to launch into a full-scale harmony.

Molly risked a glance at her grandma, whose eyes widened in alarm at the thought of what the sheep might do next. *Not Baa Baa Black Sheep! They were rehearsing that this morning.* The sheep drew a deep breath, but before they could break out into song, Molly blurted out the first thing that crossed her mind.

"Well, donkeys often wear hats when they have seaside pictures taken, so Donald got used to doing that. Then the sheep became jealous, and one day, one of them managed to acquire a beret..."

Mr. Bennet turned and stared at Molly. The sheep deflated behind him.

"Yes, yes," he snapped. "Maybe it's something else then. But something is... odd here and I'm going to find out what it is." He glanced down at the list once more. "We will start with the chicken house!" Mr. Bennet turned on one pristine wellington boot and marched off to the chicken coop, clutching the clipboard to him like a medieval shield.

"Sheep," he muttered to himself as he strode away. "Sheep in hats. Whatever next."

CHAPTER FOUR

The Inspection

Molly scampered ahead of the rest of the group and reached the chicken coop before them. She stopped at the entrance and peered into the darkness. The rancid smell of chicken poop hung in a faint cloud at the entrance, but Molly had got used to it years ago and barely noticed it now. She added "cleaning the coop" to her mental list of Things To Do, after - calming down the chicken, finding Winston, and mending the sweater. Oh, and surviving the inspection.

"Bella!" she said, in a loud whisper. "Bella! They're coming." The shadowy chicken in the corner merely sniffed pointedly and turned her head away. "There's no time for that," said Molly. "Mr. Bennet is on the warpath this morning and looking for any reason at all to put a big X on his inspection form." She stuck her head through the opening and wriggled in as far as she could go. *Not bad*, she thought, *looks normal.*

Neatly lined nests concealed the snapshots of Robbie the Rooster. Bella must have seen the red flashing lights go off, even in the gloom of the coop. Her strategically placed tail feathers covered the "We Love Robbie" poster.

"Good job," said Molly. "I'm sorry Bella, I will sort out your sweater, I promise, let's get through this inspection first." Bella rewarded her with a stony glare and a brief nod. Breathing a deep sigh of relief, and instantly regretting it as the stink of chicken poop filled her lungs, Molly backed out of the space and straight into a pair of green wellington boots.

"I'm so sorry, Mr. Bennet. I was looking for one of our chickens. She's taking a nap in here."

Mr. Bennet's beady eye fixed on Molly and his brow wrinkled.

"A nap? At this time of day? Surely this is not part of the routine. It is entirely the wrong time of day for a chicken to be sleeping. It will interfere with egg production." He tapped the Clipboard with the clicky pen impatiently. "Or is she, by any chance, ill? Have you had any cases of ridiculous chicken disease in the last year? There have been no reports from this establishment of fowl flu. Have you neglected to report them?"

"Oh, my dear me, no, no. No, Mr. Bennet, it's nothing like that at all. Our chickens are perfectly healthy," said Mrs. Flabbergast, catching up with them at last and overhearing Mr. Bennet's questions. "Nothing at all like that. No, Bella needed extra nap time today, because... because..."

"Because she laid two extra eggs this morning," interrupted Molly, holding up two fingers. "Bella is a Brown Leghorn and one of our best layers, but even she was slightly worn out after three eggs in one morning."

"Three?" gasped Mr. Bennet. "That is rather a lot. Let me check my list. It seems... unusual. Is she usually unusual, this chicken of yours?"

"Oh no, Mr. Bennet, not at all. She got a bit excited because she heard you might be visiting today and wanted to impress you." Mrs. Flabbergast smiled shyly up at him. "Bella is a big fan of yours," she said, stretching the truth like a giant elastic band.

The inspector puffed out his chest and tipped his bowler hat further back on his head. "Well, of course, any chicken of sense.... Mfff. Of course. Very good of her to try. Very good. I'll pop my head in then and say hello."

In went his head through the chicken coop door, which left the rest of him outside the chicken coop and rather vulnerable to the remaining animals. Of course, if you know anything about goats and their rather naughty sense of humor, you can imagine what thoughts ran through the goat's mind as he stood watching Mr. Bennet. Ten feet behind Mr. Bennet's rather bony backside, Jinks' eyes glittered with mischief and he started to paw the ground with one impatient hoof. No goat could resist the sight of an unguarded target as obvious as Mr. Bennet sticking out of the hen house. Head down, sharp pointy horns to the front, and Jinks was ready to charge.

Molly turned to see the first hoof hit the ground and mud splash through the air.

"Jinks! No!" she yelped, diving towards the grinning goat. Her arms wrapped around his neck and they slid to the ground in a tangle of legs and hooves and horns. Jinks bleated in frustration as his promising target backed out of the coop. Legs tangled and face in the mud, he had missed his chance.

Mr. Bennet removed his upper half from the coop, still trying not to breathe in the smell of angry chicken and stared in surprise at the small pile up behind him. "What on earth are you doing down there?" he asked.

"Just checking for ... for.... eggs," said Molly quickly.

"I think you'll find that goats don't lay eggs, young lady," said Mr. Bennet. "You'd do better to stick with the chickens for that." With the air of someone who has distinctly superior knowledge about chickens than anyone else present, Mr. Bennet nodded briefly, ticked the clipboard, and strode off sharply to the stables. A beak poked out of the doorway and Bella watched from the shadows as the noisy gaggle of animals and humans left.

Molly staggered up from the ground. Slimy, blackish mud oozed everywhere - up her nose, in her ears, round her mouth. *That wasn't funny.*

"What on earth do you think you were doing?" she asked the goat, angrily tugging at his left leg to pull him up. As it slipped from her grasp, she reached for the back of his neck and yanked him up to standing that way.

"How dare you try to upset Mr. Bennet? We need that license. Remember? Knocking him flying is bound to annoy him more than you can ever imagine. That was a terrible idea, Jinks. Don't ever do that again!"

Jinks hung his head and looked at her sadly through his long eyelashes.

"I'm so sorry, Molly. I wasn't thinking. I was goating. Like a goat. I promise never to do it again."

With his apology done with, Jinks harrumphed happily and clip clopped off after the rest of the gang. Molly shook her head and followed.

"Goating," she repeated with a grin.

***

Mr. Bennet headed for the next item on his list. The stables were home to Hampton and Donald. A ramshackle block at the end of the farmyard cobbled together with various sheets of wood and a few old doors. Jinks had designed it from what they could scrounge together, and Molly had hammered it into place as quickly as possible after Hampton had arrived to live at the farm. The longest part of it all was waiting for the planning permission from the Council.

It wasn't pretty, it didn't even really look like proper stables, but Hampton and Donald were more than happy to call it home.

Hampton was a magnificent carthorse who towered over everybody else on the farm, including Mrs. Flabbergast. His glossy black coat tapered down to the long white feathering which covered his enormous feet. The proud blaze of white on his forehead glowed and his mane had been neatly braided for the next day's recording at the studio.

Hampton stood proudly to attention in his stall, waiting. Eyes forward, head up and hooves together, he always enjoyed a good inspection.

The stable door banged open and a disheveled donkey exploded into the room. Donald had rushed ahead of the rest of the group as they had detoured to inspect the chicken coop. He barreled in, his smoky gray back hitting the sides of the door frame as he pushed through. The whole stable wobbled.

Donald pushed through his stall door and pulled it shut behind him. He pulled a great chunk of straw off the feed basket and started chewing loudly. His nostrils flared as he remembered the sheep.

"All ready and correct sir!" Hampton rested his chin on the stall divider. "Are you up to snuff sir?"

Donald carried on chomping his straw and slowly looked around at Hampton. He pawed the ground and snorted.

"Well, I am," he said. The sharp tone in his voice surprised Hampton. His friend was a gentle creature, docile and friendly, and there weren't many things which could upset him like this. "I did what Molly asked and hid all my hats. Even my special straw hat with the yellow sunflower. I didn't want to, but I followed instructions." His nostrils flared as he spoke.

"Did somebody else not follow orders then? Rebellion in the ranks, is that it?"

Donald stomped the ground. "Those sheep. Those sheep were wearing their fancy berets. Parading round for all the world to see." Donald snorted and stamped his hoof again at the unfairness. Catch him risking their farm license even for the sake of his best hat. "Those sheep think they can get away with anything! When I see the alarm, I spin the board and hide all my hats. You know that. But those sheep... Grrrrrrr!"

At the sight of the flashing red light, he had indeed jumped into action and spun the board of hats round to look like a wall full of grooming brushes, stirrups and bridles, not that either of the last two were ever used on the animals at this farm. Perfectly normal looking. Beautifully clean and smelling of fresh hay. Absolutely stable like.

"Keeping the end up, Donald. You're on fine form and I'm sure Molly appreciates it. Don't worry about those sheep. She'll sort them out. We need to do our bit. Good show, old chap, and all that." Hampton whinnied encouragingly at the angry donkey.

Donald took two deep breaths to calm himself down and restore his inner peace. He would deal with those silly sheep later.

He nodded slowly at Hampton. "All set, Captain." They stared straight ahead at the stable door, waiting for the invasion to begin.

***

Mr. Bennet strode into the stable ahead of the rest of the group, kicking up clouds of straw as he entered. Molly and Mrs. Flabbergast followed, discreetly checking that everything was in order. Molly's smile brightened. Everything looked perfectly presentable.

Except for the bright yellow silk flower sticking straight out from behind one edge of the board. The silk flower from Donald's absolutely favorite straw hat. Molly's eyes widened as she caught sight of it. *That looks completely out of place. Sticks out like a sore thumb.* She sidled along the front of the stalls to Donald's door.

"Donald..." she said, keeping her voice as low as possible. "Donald..."

The donkey carried on munching as he raised his head from the straw net. Molly nodded very slightly towards the yellow embarrassment behind him.

He stopped chewing and looked towards the board. "Oh no," he said. Thinking quickly, Donald clattered round to face the silk sunflower and, at the same time, stuck his rump in Mr. Bennet's direction and let out a particularly donkey-like smell. The cloud of stink hit Mr. Bennet in the face like an accelerating truck.

His hands flew up to cover his nose. The

clipboard and the clicky pen went flying across the stable. The bowler hat slid sideways, revealing a patch of slicked down black hair.

"Control that donkey!" he sputtered and grabbed for the neatly refolded handkerchief in his breast pocket. "He can't do that to a Farmyard and Animal Husbandry Government Inspector! It's not allowed!"

He clamped the whitish square uselessly over his nose and flapped his spare hand pathetically at the donkey's rear end. Unfortunately, it was the same handkerchief he had used earlier to wipe mud off his chin. He smeared more mud all over his nose and cheeks and forehead.

"Arrgghghh! That's revolting!" he groaned through the handkerchief.

"There, there," said Grandma. "Donald's only doing what donkeys do." She calmly picked up the clicky pen and clipboard and handed them back to the upset Inspector, without mentioning the mud streaks now covering his reddened face. "It's nothing personal Mr. Bennet. How about we go along and have a nice cup of tea and a slice of my lovely treacle and beetroot tart?"

But Mr. Bennet refused to be distracted.

"No, thank you," he said coldly. "We will press on. I will see the whole of this farm today, and even stinky donkeys will not stop me!" He turned abruptly and marched out of the stables, completely failing to notice the bright yellow flower which hung sadly from Donald's mouth. So, press on they did.

CHAPTER FIVE

Operatic Pigs

Mr. Bennet strode fearlessly across the muddy puddles and sludge paths to the pig pen. The suspiciously clean pig pen, to Mr. Bennet's way of thinking anyway.

"Why is this pig pen so tidy?" he demanded. "It should be muddy and wet and filled with scraps of food. What kind of pigs do you keep in here? It says here," jabbing at The Clipboard, "that there should be exactly 2.93 pigs per twenty square feet of pig pen, and they should have at least half a bale of straw per week. You appear to have only two pigs in this pen and they have at least three whole bales of hay. It's a monstrous waste of resources!"

Rosemary and Lavender, the two pigs in question, stared up at him. They could see nothing wrong at all with their living conditions. Pigs of their caliber, they reasoned, should not be treated like regular porcine creatures. Their specialty was opera singing, which made them a very high-class sort of creature indeed.

Molly heard the whispering as she reached the pig pen. It came from about knee level and luckily Mr. Bennet hadn't yet noticed.

"What does he mean - reduce our straw? The very thought of it! We have only just negotiated an increase in dandelion rations. Jumped up little man - who does he think he is?"

"I know, dear. I do think we should have held out for four cleanings a week instead of two, but the dandelions were worth it." Rosemary snuffled at the thought of the juicy yellow flowers, served on fine bone china together with Earl Grey tea for breakfast every morning.

"And why should it be muddy? I only require a small amount of mud for my weekly face pack."

"I think he expects us to roll in it, dear."

"Sounds revolting."

Mr. Bennet glowered at the two occupants of the pen over the edge of his clipboard. He tapped the clipboard with the clicky pen and waggled his eyebrows.

"Your pigs are too clean!" he finally announced. "Pigs should be muddy." The pigs were, indeed, cleaner than Mr. Bennet at this point.

The snorts from the pen grew louder. The ladies were not happy at all with that suggestion. "Those pigs are performing pigs," Mrs. Flabbergast said.

"We have to keep them clean in case they have to perform at short notice. Do you know how long it takes to wash off a mud-covered pig?"

Twenty-seven minutes per pig, thought Molly. *And that's when they're cooperating.*

Mr. Bennet did not know, but Mr. Bennet did not care either. He wanted everything on the farm to conform to his list. His goal - to tick off all the boxes on his list.

"You must muddy these pigs immediately and remove the extra straw," he said. "They must act like pigs in order to be counted as pigs. You must spray water into this pen to make better mud or I will not tick this box!" He jabbed the clicky pen at the clipboard. "We must have muddy pigs!" he declared. "No mud, no tick, no license!"

Mr. Bennet was immovable. Mrs. Flabbergast pleaded with him. Molly begged him. The pigs huffed their displeasure. But Mr. Bennet would not back down. Eventually Mrs. Flabbergast dragged the coil of hosepipe across the yard to the pig pen and reluctantly began to unwind it.

"They won't be happy about this you know," she warned.

"No, but I will, Mrs. Flabbergast, I will," said Mr. Bennet, looking anything but happy.

Mrs. Flabbergast attached the hose to the standing tap and turned the squeaky old handle until it opened fully. A pathetic drip dribbled through the end of the hose.

"Are you making fun of me?" Mr. Bennet's nostrils widened and his eyes bugged out. "Just do as you're told and turn it on!"

Molly looked along the length of the hosepipe as it snaked around the yard. A well-placed hoof blocked the water from making its way through the hosepipe. *This is not going to end well,* she thought.

"Jinks!" she said to the owner of that hoof. "Jinks - no!"

In a low voice, the naughty goat replied. "Oh yes, Molly!"

As Mr. Bennet peered down the hosepipe, Jinks saw his chance. Looking straight at Molly, with the most innocent expression a goat can muster, he lifted his hoof.

All the pent-up water rushed up the hosepipe at once and caught Mr. Bennet right in the face. He let go of the pipe and it danced like a crazy snake in figures of eight. The water sprayed up his nose. It soaked his dirty suit. Mud splatters fountained up wherever it hit the ground. Liquid mud sprayed everywhere. Humans and animals alike were covered in splashes and splodges and streams of brown gunk.

"Mama mia!" cried out Lavender as she ran to the fence.

"O dolce mia!" said Rosemary, squealing as a splatter of mud hit her pink scrubbed cheek and dribbled down. She flew after Lavender. They both crashed into the fence then bounced back into a huge puddle of sludge. Splosh. Splat. Yuck.

"Ew!" they both yelled and scrambled out of the mud pit. Straw and mud and potato peelings flew all over the place as they tore in circles around the pen, squealing and screaming angrily.

Jinks jumped onto the gatepost in one easy stride, bleating with laughter. That set the chickens off, pecking and clucking like angry little hammer drills.

"Oh, I say," said Hampton to Donald, as the braying and neighing and woofing and clucking built around them until it seemed that the world had gone mad. "This will not do sir. I say, it will not do!" Donald's eyes flared wide open as the sound exploded across the farmyard.

"ENOUGH!" said Mr. Bennet, his voice ringing through the storm of noise. For a moment, everyone fell silent, except for the still thrashing hosepipe. "Switch it off," he said very quietly. The tap squeaked as Mrs. Flabbergast closed it. They all turned to stare at the government inspector. He dripped from the top of his forlorn bowler hat to the bottom of his dirty wellington boots. Mud plastered his suit. His face burned red under all the mud.

I knew this wasn't going to end well, thought Molly.

Mr. Bennet clicked his pen twice and put a large cross on the top of his paperwork. "I think we can say that you have failed the inspection," he said, his voice cold and clipped.

Nobody moved. The pale sun hid behind a cloud above them and the air chilled. The silence spilled across the farmyard.

"But why?" asked Molly eventually. "What have

we ever done to upset you? Why do you always pick on us?" Her voice sounded small in the silence.

"Oh, it's not me," said Mr. Bennet. "It's my job to follow the forms, tick the boxes, obey the rules. No, it's your neighbors who don't like you and your animals."

"Our neighbors?" said Mrs. Flabbergast. "But we've always got on very well with them. We share the manure and the eggs and.... You don't mean those neighbors, do you?"

"Your next door neighbors. The Henderson family are very unhappy about the state of your backyard," repeated Mr. Bennet. "They do not like all the noise and the smells. They have made multiple complaints that you have broken the rules and are lowering the tone of the neighborhood."

"But we've put up ten-foot fences to stop the sounds getting out. We planted huge flowering bushes to keep the smells in. Haven't we Molly?" Molly nodded frantically.

"Nevertheless..." When a grownup says "nevertheless", you know that they have no intention of losing the argument, even when they don't have a leg to stand on. Mr. Bennet was as much of a grown-up as you can imagine, despite all the mud, and he enjoyed the word "nevertheless".

"We have all our permits and licenses and certificates. You have inspected us every month for the last seventeen years. What else could they possibly want?" Mrs. Flabbergast asked.

"They want you, all of you, to move out," said Mr. Bennet.

"To move out?" said Mrs. Flabbergast. "But this is our home. Where would we go?"

"To the countryside," said Mr. Bennet. "The countryside is full of animals, I believe. You would fit right in."

"But we have to be here; we need to be near to the television studios, " Mrs. Flabbergast protested. "We go there nearly every day. How could we do that from the countryside?"

"That," said Mr. Bennet "is not my problem. It is yours. I am giving you one week to come up with a solution. If, at the end of that week, the Henderson family wish to proceed with their complaint, I shall reinspect your farm. I will return on Friday and if you do not pass the re-inspection, I will issue you an Order of Eviction." Satisfied with his decision, he snapped open his wet leather briefcase, put the soggy clipboard inside and snapped it back up. He unclicked the clicky pen and put it in his suit pocket.

Mr. Bennet turned on the heels of his green wellington boots and marched to the garden gate, squelching with every footstep. "One week," he said over his shoulder as he delicately gripped the lock on the gate between his fingertips. "One week," as he creaked open the old gate and pulled it shut behind him. "One short week!" he almost chuckled as he stomped into Chestnut Crescent and back to civilization, dripping mud with every step.

"Oh Grandma," said Molly. "What are we to do?"

CHAPTER SIX

Mrs. Joseph Pops Round

"I don't know, Molly. I don't suppose there's a lot we can do." Mrs. Flabbergast folded her arms over her chest and shook her head slowly. "If the Hendersons want us to leave that badly, they're going to find a way."

Molly frowned. It wasn't fair.

"Why should we be the ones leaving?" she said. "We're not the ones trying to take over the street. They're a bunch of big bullies and now they're trying to push us out."

"Is everything all right, Mrs. Flabbergast?" A thin, watery voice called over the hedge. "Did I hear that Government Inspector back again? Whatever did he want this time?"

"Hello, dear. Yes, Mr. Bennet just left. He came to tell us that the Henderson family have filed another complaint against us."

"No!" The voice sounded shocked. A chorus of neighs and baas and woofs agreed with her. The animals were not happy about the run in with Mr.

Bennet. Molly could see the top of a maroon woolly hat bobbing through the gaps in the hedge. The hat belonged to Mrs. Joseph, one of their more sympathetic neighbors.

Winston sat down heavily on Molly's foot and sighed loudly. "They're so mean," he said loudly.

Molly clapped a hand around his snout as Mrs. Joseph's head popped up above the hedge. Fortunately, she hadn't noticed that Molly's voice had sounded unusually deep for a twelve-year-old girl. The old lady nodded hello to everybody.

"What are they complaining about this time? Those nosy neighbors made my Norman lay a new garden path. We had a beautiful fresh concrete path poured from the front door down to the gate, all wibbly wobbly round the garden so you could wander through the flower beds. The Henderson family came round the day after it dried. They complained and said we had to have paving stones like everybody else. I don't like the paving stones, I keep catching the edges."

Molly felt sorry for Mrs. Joseph. The concrete path had been laid by her son, who worried about his elderly parents tripping and falling. They lived a few doors down from the Flabbergast Farm and Mrs. Joseph frequently popped round for a cup of tea. She even braved some of Mrs. Flabbergast's baking, on occasion. Anyone who did that deserved a nice path, in Molly's opinion.

"That's not nice of them," said Molly's grandma. "What business is it of theirs what you have in your garden?"

"Oh, we're not the only ones they've had a go at." Mrs. Joseph began to work up some steam. "They made Miss Thompson get rid of her garden gnome. I must admit, he wasn't particularly to my taste. Did you see him? He held a fishing pole and couldn't keep his trousers up. She thought he was hilarious. Won him at the church fair, I believe. Anyway, they yelled at Miss Thompson until she hid her little gnome away at the bottom of the back garden. I know she's a bit of a mouse, but those Hendersons are too bossy. Thinking they know what's best for the neighborhood."

Mrs. Flabbergast leaned forward and lowered her voice. "I heard that Mrs. Henderson made Bob, at number 5, pull out his beautiful yellow rose bushes. That devastated him. Those roses were his pride and joy. They were about to pop out into a late bloom too."

"That doesn't surprise me, Mrs. Flabbergast. I understand that Mrs. Henderson can't bear to see yellow roses. They remind her of her childhood."

"How strange. Of course, she has an unnatural aversion to red front doors too. Says they're unlucky. She nagged Mr. Brawshank endlessly until the poor dear repainted his blue."

"Then Mr. Henderson turned up the next day to make him take his bird feeder down. Said they didn't want to encourage vermin in Chestnut Crescent. The cheek of it." The maroon hat tutted across the garden gate. "Do you remember when they sent letters out about the shade of roof tiles and the need for all chrysanthemums to be a uniformly rusty red color? All sorts of rubbish about 'lowering the tone of the neighborhood' and 'not letting it go downhill.' Cheek, I tell you."

The Hendersons managed to always find something to take offense to. Everything that other people did, of course. When it came to their own house, nothing was too much trouble. As soon as the solar panels had been added to the roof, they started planning the extension to the back bedroom. A sunroom appeared one summer at the attached to the side of the kitchen, and a nifty little shed in the garden the following year. Every few months, the neighbors watched gloomily as the Henderson house grew, room by room, until it towered over the rest of the Crescent.

"It's not fair," grumbled Mrs. Joseph. "I want my path back. If they can have a sunroom.... Oh hello, Ravi."

Another head, lower down, popped over the gate and leaned into the garden. Ravi Shah grinned at Molly and waved so hard he nearly tipped over the top of the gate. He was eight, very nearly nine, and lived three doors down at number 10, with his Mum and Dad and a gaggle of little sisters who adored him. Ravi was very good at helping out with egg collection when Molly ran out of time, and he was a regular visitor on the farm.

"Hi Molly. Hey there, Mrs. Flabbergast. Mum wanted me to say thank you for the manure for the garden. It's pretty stinky, but Mum loves it - says it brings the veggies up a treat."

"You're welcome, Ravi. We always have plenty of

manure for our neighbors. There's plenty to go around, dear." Mrs. Flabbergast beamed at the scruffy figure. "Did you work out what day you wanted to hold your birthday party?"

"Yeah, the fourteenth, if that's OK. It's a Saturday. Can we really ride Donald and Hampton round the Crescent? My mates will be so impressed."

"Donkey and horse rides are our specialty. Jinks loves to join in too, if you don't mind a friendly goat helping. We have to keep him away from the birthday cake, though - he loves the icing. Does two o'clock sound good?"

"Perfect, Mrs. Flabbergast. I'll let Mum know and we'll send out the invites. Thanks Mrs. Flabbergast. Bye Molly!" With one last grin, Ravi slid down from the gate and disappeared. The sound of trainers slapping the pavement gradually faded.

"Such a sweet boy," said Mrs. Joseph. "So nice of you to let him have his party here - the kids have such a marvelous time."

"We do what we can, Mrs. Joseph. Let's just hope we're still here by the 14th."

"By the way, I wondered if you had any eggs this morning."

"Of course. Why don't you come on through to the kitchen? I've baked a celery and treacle tart this morning. We can have a nice cup of tea with it."

"That would be lovely dear. Then you can tell me all about that dreadful Inspector and those nasty neighbors."

CHAPTER SEVEN

Meet the Fairy Grotto

Mrs. Flabbergast beckoned to her friend. Together they trudged into the kitchen to put the kettle on for a nice cup of tea.

She's walking slower than usual, thought Molly. Head bowed, and shoulders drooped. Normally her grandmother marched from pen to stable, coop to pond with firm strides and head held high. *I guess this really is more serious than usual.*

Molly watched them until the kitchen door clicked quietly shut. She turned and slipped away from the others. Only Freya noticed. Cats notice everything. Her eyes squeezed to thin slits as she watched her friend slink away.

The other animals gradually muttered and grumbled their ways back to their various corners of the farmyard.

Eventually Freya stood, stretched along the length of her spine, and jumped down from her perch, carefully avoiding the puddles of mud. She picked up each paw carefully in turn and placed it on the driest part of the ground, silently following Molly's path. Freya's nose twitched with distaste at the flecks of mud speckling her paws, but she felt duty bound to keep an eye on her girl, wherever she went. Even if that meant mud.

Molly slouched down the slate lined path. The path led behind the paddock and the pig pen, past the half-abandoned vegetable bed. She sank into the weather-beaten wooden chair underneath the oak tree. Her finger traced the faded gray arm of the chair, cool to her touch. It had been here as long as she could remember. Her safe place; a small oasis of peace in a home full of chaos and noise and smells and constant movement.

At her feet sat the Fairy Grotto she had built with her grandmother when she had first come to live here. Over the years, Molly had added to it. A door here, a flowerpot there. She had built a tiny rope bridge connecting the central hill to the tree. Little plants and various weeds had sprung up in the cracks and the joins and brought life to the hodge podge of tiny buildings and shelters she had crammed into the dip under the tree.

There were miniature figures of fairies, gnomes and the odd plastic cow and elephant, left over from when she played with them there when she was younger. Of course, now she had no time to play those sorts of games.

That was for little kids. But it was fun. The huge families and their adventures. Mums, Dads, Aunties, Uncles and all sorts of cousins. Fairies and goblins, and the elephants of course.

No time for that now. Too much to do.

The rope bridge needs fixing. Molly leaned forward and touched the fraying knotted string which held it all together. *Later. At least I can fix that.* She sighed and stared through the window of the closest house at the chairs and tables on the inside. They were rickety and bent, falling apart in some places, but they were from a time when it had all been so much simpler. Or maybe she had grown more complicated.

I need more time to figure this out. What if we could make an invisible wall around the Farm? Or pirates could kidnap the Hendersons. Perhaps we could win the whole lottery and buy the entire street and only keep the nice neighbors.

But she didn't know how to create an invisible wall, and she didn't know any pirates, and her grandmother refused to gamble on lottery tickets.

"There must be a way," she muttered at the fairy hanging by one wing from the tree halfway down Stardust Lane on the central hill. With one delicate finger, Molly tapped the fairy until she swung gently. "I think you should help me. What good are you lot if you can't help with some spare magic or fairy dust or something when we need you?" The fairy stayed silent, swaying uselessly from the one wing but staring at Molly with a fixed glare.

Molly glowered back, angry with everyone, even herself. "Well, you could at least try. You can't sit there pretending it won't affect you," she said. "If we have to sell the farm and move to the country, then don't think we'd bother to take you with us. Some other family would move here, and you think they would want to keep an old broken grotto like this with bits of rubbish?" Molly flicked the fairy again, making her sway more violently.

"I doubt that will help," Freya said smoothly from her perch behind Molly. The girl jumped at the sound. She hadn't heard Freya spring onto the edge of the vegetable bed.

Freya knew every sign that her girl was worried about something. From the tightness around her mouth to the way her eyes changed color from a warm blue to a curious shade of violet, Molly could never hide her worries from the wise old cat.

"I don't think anything will help," said Molly. "Why us? It's not fair! Why are they picking on us? All we try and do is give animals a good place to live. It's so unfair!"

Freya jumped down lightly onto the arm of Molly's chair and laid a gentle paw on her shoulder.

"It will be alright, Molly," she said. "If the worst comes to the worst, we'll all move out to the country and carry on there. We'll have to do longer trips into town for the television shows, but maybe we won't have to do so many."

But the tears dripped from Molly's warm cheeks like raindrops down the windowpane. Freya tried again.

"We might even be able to afford a proper farmyard," she said. "With a bigger stable for Hampton that he can turn around in, and a suitably refined pigpen for Lavender and Rosemary. That goat will want his own dressing room no doubt, with the airs he gives himself. But on the upside, we might have room for a kennel in the yard to stick that dog in."

"I can't go," sobbed Molly, her words muffled by her hands.

"I know it's hard to imagine. But we might not have a choice this time. Will it really matter that much? If we're all together, we would be fine," Freya said softly.

Molly snorted out another sob, and the tears squeezed between her fingers.

"But why would it be so awful, Molly? It's just a farm. It's who we are with that matters, isn't it? Why is it so important to you to stay here?"

The words burst out of Molly before she could stop them.

"Because if we left, my dad couldn't find us again." She buried her face in her hands again and the tears fell even harder.

"Where is he?" asked Freya softly. "You never mention him."

Slowly the crying eased, and Molly wiped her sticky nose with the back of her hand. She took a couple of shuddering deep breaths and looked hard at the fairy grotto rather than directly at Freya.

"He's somewhere out in the Middle East I think," she said. "He's a secret spy for the government. You can't tell anyone though. He lives a really exciting life out there, with car chases and helicopter rides and races over rooftops and things."

She paused to flick the fairy hanging from her one fragile wing. One small sniff escaped. Molly clenched her jaw tightly for a second, trying to hold it all together long enough to finish explaining. Her gaze stayed fixed on the gently swaying fairy.

But that's why he can't get home. He can't tell us where he is.

He can't even write. It's too dangerous.

So, if we move, he might not find us again.

We can't leave.

I have to stop them making us move. But how?

She sniffed a loud snort to stop the tears coming again and risked a look at Freya. "Please don't tell the others."

The cat considered. Her jade green eyes narrowed and the tip of her tail flicked from left to right and back again. She didn't know what to make of the story about her dad, but she did know Molly had missed something important.

"What makes you think you have to do this by yourself?" she asked. "You know you're not on your own here. We'll do this together."

"Oh, I know," said Molly, but she sank lower into the chair and her eyes were still fixed on the abandoned grotto.

"No." The tail flicked again. "This isn't all your problem. There are how many of us living here together? And not all of us have the intellectual ability of a chicken. I think we should be able to come up with a plan to thwart those nasty neighbors if we put our heads together."

"That's not very nice to chickens," Molly said.

"Well, roosters then."

"Fair enough," agreed Molly. "And the thwarting sounds fun." A weak smile twitched at her mouth.

"We're a family, Molly. We should at least all try together. We can't let you lose hope of seeing your dad again. Why don't we get everything together and see what we can come up with? What do you say?"

Molly stared at the fairy grotto again. A germ of an idea poked its way into her mind. A small suggestion, an inkling of a thought. Something about the rotting, broken old fairy grotto began to suggest a possible solution. Her shoulders lifted slightly, and she raised her head with a more determined look than Freya had expected.

Freya hated to see Molly give up on things. The sleek black cat felt more relieved than she had realized to see the fire come back.

"Let's get them all together. But not Grandma. She must be kept out of this. She believes in the system, and the licenses, and the Mr. Bennets of this world with their clipboards and their clicky pens. I don't want her to get in to trouble if it all goes wrong. If she doesn't know, she can't be blamed if it all goes wrong. Agreed – no grandma?"

"If you insist. But we should get a move on. We don't have much time." Freya jumped elegantly down from the arm of the chair and stretched her full length. "I'll round them up."

CHAPTER EIGHT

Emergency Meeting

Hooves stomped and feathers ruffled as all the animals found a good place to perch or stand. Robbie the Rooster took pride of place on top of Donald's stall door. His chickens chattered on the floor in front of him. He looked over them proudly as they settled their feathers and gathered their wits for the meeting.

"Settle down ladies, there's plenty of room for you all. Can everybody see me okay down there? Cool, cool. I'll be signing autographs after the meeting, ladies, and I have new pictures from my last photo shoot to hand out to all of you." Robbie strutted along the top of the door, back and forth, counting his chickens and showing off his tail feathers.

"Has anyone seen Bella today?" The chickens all clucked and fussed, jealous of Bella being singled out for attention. "Bella?" he called out, his crowing loud enough to be heard at the other end of the pig pen. But Robbie couldn't see her anywhere.

"We need her here ladies. She's the smartest chicken of all. Does anybody know where she is? No, well, I'll have to go and look for her then. Excuse me, excuse me…" Robbie flapped his strong wings and nearly toppled off the top of the stable door as he reared up. "Must go and find my Bella," he called.

This sort of favoritism from their rock star hero was unheard of. The chickens cackled angrily as he tried to find a space to jump down into.

"She'll be here when she feels like it," said one.

"That Bella's always late," shouted out another.

"She's too snooty to hang out with us," called another. "We're not good enough for her. Don't waste your time, Robbie. We love you!"

"Yes, we love you!"

"Stay here, Robbie – give us your latest hit!" They crowded round him, pushing closer and closer until the world seemed filled with chickens. They jostled each other in the tight space, beaks raised to their hero, calling out for a song from him.

"I want to hear 'Crowing to the Stars'!" shouted the first chicken, pushing right to the front of the crowd with a dreamy eyed look in her eye.

"No – 'Pecking around the Clock' is my favorite!" The argument grew louder and louder until none of it made any sense.

In the stable doorway, a small shadowy figure appeared. She looked down her beak at the battling chickens, then stared at the frustrated rooster.

"Ladies!" shouted Robbie. He crowed long and loud. Everybody froze in position and looked at him.

"Bella's here. Make some room at the front for my number one fan." He winked at the surprised chicken and hopped back up to his perch.

***

Donald, his straw hat flopping over one beechnut colored eye, rested his chin over the stall. He moistly chewed a good mouthful of straw and watched the chicken chaos with a philosophical air. In Donald's opinion, some animals were sensible, and some were plain chicken crazy. He generally preferred the ones who walked on all four legs. They appeared to be a lot more stable than the others, apart from Jinks, of course.

His one exception to the rule was Molly. Remarkably intelligent for a two legged being, in his view. That and she had a good eye for when a donkey needed brushing down properly. Yes, Molly is absolutely fine, thought Donald.

"Are you taking roll call there?" Hampton loomed over Donald by several hands. "We should keep track of our visitors, Donald. It's an honor to be the venue for such an important meeting. By golly, yes sir, it is. Are you counting them all in Donald?"

"I'm watching," said the donkey, in his soft drawling voice. "Do you think they'll all fit in here

Captain?" he asked. "It's not a big stable."

"I remember when we could all fit into the kitchen for meetings," said Hampton. "Quite a while ago now, I suppose. But things were better organized in those days. Now, well, chickens everywhere, young Donald, chickens everywhere." There were, indeed, quite a few chickens underfoot. But they weren't the only ones. The other animals had started arriving as well, and the stable began to fill up. Donald and Hampton nodded politely to each animal as they entered the stable.

Daisy, their rare red and white Dairy Shorthorn cow, sauntered in and swayed over to Donald's stall.

"Good afternoon, Donald," she said, nodding briefly at him. "Delightful to see you again Captain," - she batted her long dark eyelashes at Hampton in the next stall over. "So pleasant to have these little afternoon gatherings." Donald rolled his eyes at Hampton. Daisy's airs and graces were a source of great entertainment to the two of them, but they never dared make jokes about her to her face. An upset cow can cause considerable damage to a confined space like a stable.

"Do come and stand here, Daisy," said Hampton, trying not to laugh as she wiggled her way over to his stall. Her enormous backside swung back and forth, and her tail knocked over a chicken as she crossed the floor.

***

"Make room, make room." In quacked Duck, with a great flapping of wings. "Right, where shall I sit?" she fussed. "I need to be at the front. Budge up you silly chickens; there should be room for all of us. Winston, come and sit with me." Duck looked like any other dappled brown duck you might meet on a farm, apart from two things. Firstly, the talking part, which might be considered unusual. Secondly, she wore a bright blue headband across her forehead, which matched the flash of blue on her wings. She was, in fact, a Ninja Duck, who had trained in martial arts before she arrived at the farm. Nobody knew why, and Duck never could sit still long enough to explain it to them.

Winston bumbled over to where Duck had pushed the chickens out of the way. "Nice of you, Duck. Have you met the new puppies? This here is George, and this is Martha. Or is it Martha and George? Will you two sit down and behave or I'll be in even more trouble. Molly will think I can't even control two silly puppies."

"Yes Winston, sorry Winston," chorused the two blond bundles of muddy fur that skidded to a halt beside him.

"Started their training yet Winston?" asked Duck. "They're never too young, y'know. I myself started martial arts training when I was a fluffy duckling. Oh yes, you should send the puppies over to me. We'll soon have them trained with round legs and front kicks and haikus and things like that."

"To be honest, Duck, I don't know if it's worth it.

I mean, look at them. They can't even sit down without falling over each other. What would be the point of teaching them to fall over dangerously? They're more likely to hurt themselves than a burglar?"

"That's not the attitude, my old friend. We need to put together an army. An army of animals to fend off those neighbors. That's what Molly's called the meeting about, you can be sure of that. She's going to raise a platoon of armed animals to defend the farm and stop them kicking us out. I will lead the charge! No enemy too great, no invader too big. I will lead us all to victory!" Duck's wings flapped with each declaration, until she rose up from the floor with determined enthusiasm.

"Ninja Duck to the fore!" she cried. "I will lead us into battle!" Duck turned a complete circle and kicked out sideways with one webbed foot. It caught Winston squarely on the nose and he yelped.

"Do you mind, Duck?"

"Sorry, Winston, got to keep in shape though. Have to stay fighting fit. Keep your wits about you, that sort of thing. Watch me, young pups, I'll show you how it's done."

CHAPTER NINE

Called to Order

Gradually the stables filled up with not only the animals, but also their sounds and their smells. The sheep shoved their way through the growing crowd and filled the corner opposite the door. They had names, but only Molly could tell them apart. Mrs. Flabbergast called them all "You sheep." They did everything as a group, from grazing to moving around the farmyard, and looked as if a particularly solid, and muddy, cloud had dropped from the sky to form a block of wiry wool.

As if they were many sheep with one controller, they stuck their heads up in the air and launched into song.

"Baaaaaa, baaaaaaa, blaaaaaack sheeeeeeppp...."

"Do keep it down," shouted Hampton, towering over them all from his stall. "This is not the music hall, y'know." But the sheep went on, oblivious. They had barely even noticed the trouble they had caused with their blue berets and wouldn't have cared anyway.

"Haaaave you aaaaany woooool..." they warbled, ignoring the loud mutterings from the animals around them.

Larry, the lone llama on the farm, trotted in and stood next to them, proudly displaying his reclaimed purple feather boa, wrapped from the top to the bottom of his long neck. His booming baritone voice joined the choruses, slightly flat and a beat or two late and earning himself some unpleasant stares from the sheep.

***

The stables appeared to be full to the rafters, but then the two enormous pigs arrived. Rosemary and Lavender pushed their way through the crowd to their rightful place at the front. The mud had dried and cracked on their soft pink skins and, despite their best efforts to clean each other up, the dirt had stuck everywhere.

"I don't know why you made me come," said Rosemary as they pushed their way past the wriggling geese.

"We can't miss a meeting like this," replied Lavender. "They couldn't possibly make the right decisions without us."

"But look at the state of us. Mud everywhere.

Bits of straw. My tail is still uncurled, and you have an inside out ear. They could have waited for us to clean up."

"I don't think we have that long dear; it's going to take all day to do that, and this is a teeny bit more urgent."

"How on earth can you say that? We look like we live in a - a - a pigsty."

"I know," said Lavender, trying not to lose her patience, "but a pig must do what a pig must do. Look, we can hide at the back behind the chickens and no one will notice that we're a touch disheveled." Rosemary snorted in reply.

"Is everyone here?" asked Molly. She clambered carefully over a puppy, two chickens and round a sheep to get to the front of the herd. The animals all glanced around but the dense crowd made it impossible to see everyone clearly. "Freya - who are we missing?"

"Well, you're here, and I'm here. Unfortunately, so is that dog. But you can't have everything." Molly frowned at the cat and folded her arms in disapproval.

Freya went on. "So that's the most important people accounted for," the cat said, licking one paw and rubbing it roughly over her ear. She paused to look around. "Unless you want that goat of course."

"Jinks! Of course!" said Molly. "We need Jinks. He always has the craziest ideas, but sometimes they are the best ones. Where is he? Jinks!" she called.

The goat stuck his head up from the feeder in

Donald's stall and clambered up onto a bale of straw to lean over the stall divider. "Hmmmmm?" he said, chewing loudly on a mouthful of Donald's hay.

"Good. Now we can get started," said Molly. "Now, you all heard the problem. We need to find a way to make the Hendersons change their minds about us. Or for Mr. Bennet to suddenly become our best friend and tick every box he can find on his Clipboard." She glanced nervously at Freya. *Please don't mention my dad.* Freya gave a small nod. Molly went on.

"We can't let them kick us out of our home and away into the country. It would upset Grandma no end to leave this place, with all her memories here. We have to stop it now. Does anyone have any ideas?"

"We should write to the King," said Lavender, her mud-covered nose high in the air. "He would surely intervene on our behalf."

"Oh absolutely," Rosemary snorted in agreement. "He would understand precisely how superior pigs like us should not be subjected to this sort of stress."

"Oh, yes, yes, super idea," said Winston. "Wish I'd thought of that," he muttered quietly. George and Martha woofed gently in agreement and nodded alongside him.

"Or the Head of the BBC," suggested Donald. "He greatly admired my hat the last time I saw him in the lift. He knows how vital our work is to the smooth running of the nation's television productions. Couldn't do it without us, of course. I'm sure he would have a word with Mr. Bennet for us and it would all be sorted out in no time."

"Hear, hear!" said Winston. George and Martha woofed their agreement too. Winston patted them gently on the tops of their heads and smiled. Then a thought struck him. "Actually," he said slowly, "I wonder."

"What?" said Molly, keen to hear any sensible idea.

"We could send George and Martha to go and live with him for a while and turn him into an animal lover. Two weeks with these two, and he'll be willing to sign any license we put in front of him."

Molly tilted her head to one side and thought about it. Her hand wandered to her braid and she tugged it gently as she considered the idea. *Maybe not as ridiculous as some of the other ideas, but probably not extreme enough to stop the Hendersons,* she thought.

"Don't be so daft," snapped the cat at her side. Freya didn't see the appeal of puppies - such messy, noisy things. Always getting into trouble. Not like her own adorable kittens. "Who would like animals after having to live with dogs?"

Winston's head sank and he lay down on the floor. Molly put her hand on Freya's head and said quietly "That's enough. He wanted to help."

"It was a stupid idea," said the cat. Molly flicked a disapproving glance her way, but Freya stuck her nose up and turned away haughtily.

"Anyone else?" asked Molly hopefully.

"I could eat his hat," offered Larry the Llama. "Even though I expect it tastes nasty." The other animals all nodded, even the sheep.

"I've seen you eat an umbrella," said Molly in surprise.

"Yes, but he smells of pine trees. Why would a human want to smell like a tree?"

"Oh no," said Molly with a giggle, "that's just his aftershave. I expect he thinks that's what a government inspector should smell like."

"Like a prickly tree?" repeated Larry, going a little cross-eyed at the thought. "What a strange human."

"We could put it on Robbie's fan club page," chimed in one of the chickens.

"Ooh, yes, we could start a petition and then advertise it on his web page. Everyone would pay attention then," said another. The chickens got so excited they started chattering and pecking the ground so noisily that Molly couldn't be heard. Robbie looked down proudly over his ladies for a minute, then emitted a ringing cock-a-doodle-do. They all looked up at him admiringly and fell silent.

"It could be done," he conceded. "But even all my fans might not convince Mr. Bennet. I think, Molly, that we should do something about our neighbors instead." Robbie rarely said so much in one go. Molly hadn't realized he had been paying that much attention to the problem.

"Do you have any ideas, Robbie?"

"Ideas? I don't do ideas," he said, blinking

rapidly at the suggestion. "I'm a bird of action. Ask Jinks, he's the one for ideas."

Every head turned to the goat, chewing his breakfast for the third time. His eyes widened. Jinks quickly swallowed the mouthful and gave a loud burp of satisfaction.

"Pardon me." His eyes crossed and he grinned at the others. "Sorry, what were you saying?"

"Robbie said you might have a Plan for dealing with the Hendersons. Do you, Jinks? I wondered if we could..." *No... the fairy grotto idea... it's too vague. We need a definite Plan.* "Robbie suggested we should sort out the neighbors instead of Mr. Bennet. What do you think?"

"A Plan? Ideas? I'm sure I must have something we can use... Let me think a minute." He stepped down from his straw step, turned around several times, hit the feeder and bleated at it in surprise, then backed up against the door. The others waited patiently for him to come up with one of his Brilliant Ideas.

Jinks pushed the stall door open and trotted into the middle of the ring of animals. "I've got it. An amazing Plan. A wonderful idea. It will save us all!"

Molly's eyebrows rose and she glanced at Freya. The cat's eyes narrowed as she watched Jinks prance about. Any ideas from Jinks needed a thorough examination.

"This wouldn't be along the lines of upside-down umbrellas, painting the chickens blue, or Hampton learning to play the banjo, would it?" she asked. A roar of dissent rose from the floor. The other animals loved Jinks' ideas; no one ever knew what might happen when they tried them out.

"Go on Jinks, tell us the Plan," said Donald.

"We're all ears," said Daisy from the back corner. "Do tell us dear Jinks. We want to hear from yoooouuu..."

"Go for it!" said Winston.

"We should make them think their house is making them sick," he said, prancing and spinning with excitement. "Then they will leave, and we won't have to."

Molly and Freya looked at each other again, considering the idea from every angle. Freya nodded slowly.

"Actually, that's a pretty good idea," said Molly. "I think you may have something there Jinks. Are we all in agreement everyone?" The braying and woofing and Hear Hears were enough to tell her that they were.

***

Molly, Jinks and Freya huddled together at the end of the garden and worked out the details. They settled down on the old wooden chair, Molly on the seat, Freya on the arm and Jinks peering over Molly's shoulder.

"I came up with the idea," said the goat. "You should let me write it down."

"You may be able to talk, but I'm still the only here who can write," said Molly. She ran her finger down the page. "It's beginning to look like quite a long list already."

Freya gently patted the fairy hanging in the fairy grotto until it swung to and fro. The tiny figure had been joined by two of the dolls from Molly's dolls house, an inch high plastic soldier from a Christmas cracker, and a miniature blue china hippo sitting on its rump.

"Is this one Mr. Henderson?" Jinks could never pay attention to one idea for very long, even his own. He nudged a plastic hippo with his nose.

Freya pointed at the soldier in one of the top floor Grotto rooms. "That's him. The two dolls are the kids, and of course, Mrs. Henderson is the hippo." The figures were scattered around the various rooms of the Grotto. "See, sheds in here, in the kitchen, cooking the breakfast."

"That's where we'll get Bella to hide in the pantry and make some noises. Upstairs, where the kids are, we can put some itching powder in their underwear maybe."

The chill of the morning had seeped away, and the early afternoon sun shined down on them as they put their heads together. While the other animals got on with their training and chores, the three of them plotted the downfall of the Hendersons. Every so often, Molly glanced up at the farmhouse and saw her grandma at the kitchen sink, happily kneading the dough for a banana and pepper bread.

Jinks caught her looking. "Do you think we should tell her what we're doing?"

"No," said Molly. "Definitely not. It's best that we get on with it ourselves." She turned to Freya for support.

"I have to agree with Molly on this occasion. What would happen if it all went wrong, and her grandma was involved?"

"She'd get all the blame because she's supposed to be the grown up," said Molly. "Not that your amazing plan will go wrong of course, but if it did, it's best that she knows nothing about it. We don't want her to lose her animal license too, now do we?"

"I don't know. I think she should know what's going on. I don't like planning things behind her back. She always knows when something is going on," he said.

"This time it's for her own good." Molly waved the list under his nose to keep him focused on the matter in hand.

"So, we have the pepper shaker, itching powder, whoopee cushions and a talking chicken on the list. Is there anything else we need?" Freya and Jinks shook their heads. Molly's eyes lit up as another thought struck her. She tapped the pencil against the list in excitement. "Actually," she said, "I got a box of tricks from Mr. Mountebank's Humbug Emporium as a Christmas present. I think this may be the perfect opportunity to try out some of the things in there...." Her smile spread slowly from ear to ear.

CHAPTER TEN

Bedtime Story

The pale pink lampshade glowed warmly on the nightstand, throwing familiar shadows across the ceiling. Molly snuggled deeper into the cool sheets and puffy eiderdown, her head sinking into the soft pillow and leaving the tip of her nose visible. Her grandma bustled about, closing the curtains and picking up dirty socks and a mud splattered t-shirt.

"It'll be all right, Molly." She tried to sound reassuring, but Molly could hear a slight wobble in her grandma's voice. "We'll figure out a way to stay."

How much easier it would be if Grandma knew what we're planning, thought Molly. *But it might land her in hot water if it all went wrong. I can't let anything hurt her. It's too risky.*

"Tell me the story," she said instead, her voice soft and sleepy.

"Again?" said her grandma. "You've heard it so many times before. I could read you that new adventure story instead, if you like." She reached across to the nightstand and straightened the photo frame next to the lamp.

"No. The story," insisted Molly.

"Very well." Molly felt the bed sink on one side as her grandma settled herself on the edge of the bed, smoothing the covers and getting comfortable.

"Seventeen years ago, I had a wonderful dog called Steven living with me. A gorgeous black and white border collie with bright eyes and soft fur. Steven learned all these incredible tricks just by listening to a few instructions. He parachuted out of small airplanes, jumped through hoops of raging fire, and even brewed a good cup of tea, which a lot of people can't do.

Every Saturday night, Steven was on "Stars of the Screen" with a new trick. Every Monday morning, it was "Circus Stars". Thursday afternoons, he played the "dog by the fireside" role in "Story time". Steven got so rich and famous from all his performances that he had his own celebrity photo shoots and his own bank account. He even had a shiny red jacket with gold trim to wear whenever we went to the TV studios. We couldn't have anyone mistaking him for a normal dog.

Everyone assumed that it was my "special training techniques" that made him do those tricks. I must admit, I thought I was the bee's knees when it came to dog training. But the truth was that Steven listened very carefully. Steven knew how to listen because he knew how to talk.

But years of being adored by the public had had an effect on him. Steven loved for people to pat him and stroke him and tell him how clever he was. Vanity can lead the best of us astray, my dear Molly.

After a particularly successful training session, Steven felt that he hadn't got the praise he wanted. Juggling with hamsters was, apparently, worthy of at least three head pats and a handful of Good Boy crunchy treats. Instead, all I'd given him was a half-hearted scratch on the head and a "Whoosa a good boy then?"

He shook his head furiously and said - "I am." Luckily, no one else heard. I had been suspicious about this collie for a while.

"I knew it," I said, "I knew there was something different about you."

"The riding a unicycle and leaping tall buildings didn't give it away then?" the dog asked, cocking his head to one side. Steven always thought humans were not the cleverest creatures.

"That's just tricks," I told him. "But a TALKING dog! Think what we could do, you and me."

"Ah," said Steven. "But that's where we come unstuck, my dear lady. A talking dog is a novelty one day and a threat the next. People like to think they are the cleverest of all, and if they thought a dog could outsmart them, well, I don't like to wonder what would happen to that dog. I thought we were doing fine with the television shows. Don't you agree?" I thought about it, from every possible angle. I really did. He was right, I had to admit. But I also sniffed an opportunity for us to make our fortune, and I've never been one to give up easily.

"How did you learn to talk?" I asked him.

"Born that way." Steven shrugged. "I could always understand what humans were saying. But as a pup, I met a wise bulldog who warned me never to let on. There are a few of us who have the talent. Apart from parrots, who are too stupid to keep their big beaks shut, we all try to keep it a secret."

"There are more of you?" I was amazed.

"Well, yes. I have met a few talkers along the way." He tried to look casual about it.

"Are they all dogs?" I asked him.

"Oh no. There are all sorts – cows, sheep, pigeons, ducks, donkeys, alligators. And that's the ones I've met personally."

"Really?" We could take over all the best performing animal gigs on television and in films and maybe even the occasional Shakespearean theater role. What an exciting idea it was. "Do they understand instructions? If you tell them what to do, will they do it?" I peppered him with questions.

"Well," said Steven, thinking hard about it. "Animals tend to do what they want to do and when they want to do it. But I think we could work out a mutually beneficial system of rewards to make sure that they also do what you want them to do."

"I see," I said. But half the time I had no idea what that dog talked about. I suggested a simpler plan. "Or we could tell them what to do and give them treats when they do it." Steven rolled his eyes at me, just a little bit, but he tended to do that a lot. I remember hoping that the other talking animals weren't all as smart as Steven, or I would have trouble on my hands. But the idea had taken root, and we soon realized we could be even more successful running a team of "trained" animals.

So that's how The Flabbergast Farm and our performing animals got started. Together, Steven and I traveled the length and breadth of the country searching for more talkers. We decided early on to stay on the mainland. You know I can't do 'furrin langwiches,' apart from 'oh revur' and 'crossint'. We thought that wouldn't have got us very far. A horse talking Swedish or a German speaking duck would have been a nightmare to understand.

So we explored the whole country in my old blue Land rover. We visited farms and villages all over. Steven would start up a conversation with a random cow or have a natter with a nosy pig. Then we'd convince the animal in question to come and live with us, strike a quick deal with the unsuspecting farmer, and pretty soon the farmyard was filled to the brim with cackling, mooing, and neighing. Not to mention all the talking and shouting and chattering.

Our farm's reputation grew quickly in the world of television and film, and soon we were known for having the best trained animals in town.

As more animals joined us, we added more buildings. A stable for Hampton, and that llama's shed. I put in a coop when the chickens started arriving. The duck pond for the ducks. The cow shed for Daisy. The pig pen came later when Rosemary came to us. To tell you the truth, it started to get a bit crowded. But I found it impossible to turn away a new animal that needed a home.

Of course, seventeen years ago is an awful lot of years in dog years, and Steven died peacefully of old age several years ago. I buried him in the back corner of the farmyard in a nice sunny spot. Then, as it began to get a bit too much for one grandmother to manage by herself, a wonderful five-year-old Molly appeared on the doorstep and stayed to help." Mrs. Flabbergast smiled, lost in her memories for a moment.

A gentle snore floated up from the depths of the pillow.

CHAPTER ELEVEN

Introducing the Hendersons

Sunday afternoon was the perfect time to break into the Henderson home. The Henderson family had a strict routine every Sunday and Molly had never known them to break it yet. Four o'clock on the dot, they would go for a brisk run around the neighborhood. The point of the run was to make sure everyone could see how motivated they were, rather than actually improving their fitness.

Mr. Henderson would lead the way. Or rather, Mr. Henderson's beard would lead the way. He had one of those sorts of beards which always took charge of a room. Once that beard walked in, everyone would turn to stare at it. Mr. Henderson might possibly have been less of a bully himself if he hadn't felt so second-in-command to his beard all the time. It grew large and wide and wiry and stuck out from his chin in a determined manner. The gloriously red beard glowed as if it were on fire when the evening sun's rays caught it, as often happened on their afternoon jogs.

Nothing else about Mr. Henderson was particularly memorable, just his facial hair. His tiny ears and shrunken nose looked like they were trying to run away from the great beard, and his beady little eyes would peer angrily over that forest of wiriness. Even the hair on his head faded into a flat, greasy brown. Short and flat, shedding a constant smattering of white flakes.

Every Sunday afternoon, come rain or shine, the beard would lead them on what could have been, for any other family, a gentle family jog around the neighborhood. For the Henderson family, however, it became a forced fast march through the public thoroughfares at maximum volume. Mr. Henderson's shouted commands could be heard down the whole Crescent.

This Sunday was no different. Molly and Jinks peered over the hedge separating the two houses as the freshly painted, blue front door opened next door at exactly five o'clock. The Henderson family emerged and formed a line on the driveway.

Mr. Henderson, his daughter Petunia, her brother Alastair, and at the back of the line, Mrs. Henderson. They all wore matching white tracksuits, with identical blue t-shirts peeking out from under the jackets. Mr. Henderson, Mrs. Henderson and the ever-perky Petunia stood with straight backs and heads held high, knowing that half the street was watching them. Alastair slumped where he stood, trying to be as invisible as possible.

Petunia was her parents' pride and joy.

She thinks she's all that and then some, thought Molly. *Just 'cause she goes to that posh school. They're all the same, the girls who go there. Sappy, snorting, barking types.*

Petunia did indeed attend the Hazeldene Academy for Young Ladies on the other side of Suburbiton. Complete with a ridiculous straw boater on her head and hockey stick in her hand. Molly herself went to the local comprehensive, which fell far below Princess Petunia's standards. Only good enough for the likes of Molly.

The two schools met occasionally on the hockey field. Molly always looked forward to those games. It was a good chance to get the boot in. Or the stick, as it were.

It's not like she's nice. Or pretty. She's got her mum's huge nose and her dad's squinty eyes. And she's got no idea how to smile.

Molly's thoughts were interrupted by a harrumphing cough.

"Attention everyone," said Mr. Henderson, slightly muffled by his beard. "We'll be doing the four-mile circuit this afternoon, right past the duck pond, left at the phone box, and right at the Post Office. I expect knees to be up and chins to match. Riiiiiiight Turn!" He turned smartly and banged his heels together.

"Left, right, left, right," he bellowed. Off they

went, knees pumping and feet slapping the pavement.

"Right, left, right, left." Petunia chimed in with her father's chant.

"Oh, shut up," said Alastair behind her. He glanced about, twitching at every slight movement.

"I was helping keep time," she chirped back.

"I can hear you enjoying this. I don't know how you can, everyone watching us and all."

"They're admiring us," replied his sister. She simpered at Mrs. Joseph at number 11, leaning on her picket fence and openly staring. "Good afternoon dear, how's your arthritis?"

Mrs. Joseph muttered something under her breath and backed away rapidly.

"Silly old bat," said Petunia, not even lowering her voice. "She's only jealous."

"Give it a rest, Petunia," groaned Alastair. "Let's just get this over with and hope Dad doesn't make it twice a week. You need to stop encouraging him."

"But it's so much fun" said his sister, squeezing every ounce of irritation out of the weekly torture. Her sleek, blond ponytail swung back and forth vigorously, slapping Alastair across the face as often as she could manage it.

Behind Alastair, Mrs. Henderson completed the procession. Thin as a stick insect, or "fashionably slim" as she called it. Her knees were unpleasantly bony and looked like an engine's pistons pumping up and down as she jogged behind the other three. Her elbows moving rhythmically in time with the knees, she chirruped along with her husband's chants, ever so slightly out of time and annoying him enormously.

"One, two, one two," Henderson barked as they progressed down the street. "Knees up everybody, good for the heart!" Some neighbors twitched their net curtains aside to get a good view, others were more obvious about it. In fact, thought Alastair, an awful lot of hedge trimming, bird feeder filling and front gate painting burst into life at five o" clock on Sundays. He scowled at them all.

Normally, half the farmyard would be watching this part of the routine too, enormously entertained by the sight of the undignified procession wending their way up the street. But this afternoon, they were too busy getting ready for the part after the start of the Henderson Run. Only Molly and Jinks were watching.

Jinks whispered a countdown as the four bouncing joggers reached the end of the road and turned the corner onto Highdown Road. "Five, four, three, two, one...... Let's go!"

CHAPTER TWELVE

The Set Up

"Come on, everyone. We don't have much time. Let's go!" said Molly. *This is it,* she thought. *Time to fix those Hendersons for good.*

A variety of heads appeared at the hedge next to Jinks.

Molly opened the front gate and slipped out onto the Crescent. She beckoned to the others to follow her and headed to the gate next door.

Tiptoeing up the front path, the gang looked like they were up to no good. Which they most definitely were. Molly had a well stuffed backpack slung over one shoulder and carried a slightly battered cardboard trunk with peeling corners and a red plastic handle. "Mr. Mounteb..." was splashed across one edge of it.

"Come on you lot," she murmured. "Try to act naturally. I don't think anyone's looking, they're all busy watching "Yard Hunt" I should think. But let's be quick about it."

She wasn't quite right about this. True, nearly all the residents of Chestnut Crescent were avid viewers of that particular show during Sunday teatime. Normally, there was a mass removal to the televisions screens as soon as the Hendersons were out of sight.

However, word had got around about the trouble the Flabbergast Farm currently faced. Rumor had hopped from front garden to front garden, over fences and hedges and all the way down the street. These neighbors were less than happy about the idea of losing their resident farm.

But no one could think of a way to help Mrs. Flabbergast and Molly. They waited, and watched from behind their hedges and net curtains, to see what would happen next.

"How are we going to get in?" asked Jinks, stooping down to chew on a particularly tasty looking rose bush.

"I shall fly up to the roof, shimmy down the chimney, and let you all in through the back window," offered Duck, her ninja skills coming to her aid.

"I could peck my way in through a window at the back, if you think it's necessary," offered Bella.

"Don't be silly," said Duck. "Someone would hear the glass breaking. They'd call the Hendersons."

"That's no sillier than flying down the chimney," argued the annoyed chicken. Duck and Bella stood beak to beak, ready to fight.

"Or we could open the front door," said Molly, pushing between the two of them. "They leave a spare key under the flowerpot here."

"Why on earth would people do that?" asked Jinks. "Lock the door then leave the key for anyone to find it."

"In case they get locked out of course."

Jinks shook his head in disbelief.

"Because people are stupid," said Freya. "Except Molly," she added quickly.

"Well come on then." Winston said. "Before someone notices." He sniffed the air carefully. "And before we get wet."

Molly looked around to see if anyone could see them. The net curtains at various front windows dropped back into place as she turned. She reached down and felt under the largest flowerpot.

"Here it is," she said, pulling out the shiny silver key and inserting it quickly into the door lock. With a short jiggle, the front door swung open with a groan. She slipped the key back under the flowerpot.

"Quick, Molly, before anybody sees us," said Winston, in what he considered a whisper. His tail wagged so fiercely it nearly knocked her off the step. If anybody had been watching, they might have been slightly curious about the sight of an Old English sheepdog, a goat, a chicken, a cat and a duck following a girl into the neighbors' house. But of course, nobody would admit to looking.

Molly stepped through the door and the animals bundled her inside. None of them had ever been all the way into the house - they had only ever seen glimpses through the windows and the occasionally open door. It felt like they had entered a forbidden land.

Molly peered into the dimly lit hallway. The layout looked similar to their own house, but in reverse. In this house, the kitchen went off to the left, and the living room was on the right.

The hallway had been painted a dark green color. *Pokey*, thought Molly. *I prefer Grandma's cream-colored hallway. It feels bigger.*

Jinks nudged her into the hallway before she could change her mind, and the other animals crowded in silently behind them. The walls were absolutely crammed with pictures of the Hendersons; some in groups of the four of them, and some of them standing on their own. In others, family members stood proudly holding tennis rackets or clarinets, caressing a new BMW and in one case, wrestling an alligator.

An alligator? That seems a little.... adventurous for the Hendersons.

"That's Morris," said Winston, glancing at the picture. "He lives at the Suburbiton zoo and pretends to wrestle children. He's pretty harmless. I've run into him a few times with your grandmother."

"Oh. I see. Is he a talker too?"

"Like you wouldn't believe. He never stops talking. Does he Jinks?"

"That's right," replied the goat. "Mrs. Flabbergast has offered him a home before now, but I think we were all glad when he said no. He likes being the star of the show over at the zoo and he says the catering is superb."

Molly nodded. *I'm not even going to think about what the catering might consist of,* she thought.

"We should get a move on," said Duck. "Can't stand around looking at pictures all day." She bustled ahead of them, nudging open the door to the living room.

Photographs covered the living room too. On the walls. In miniature frames on the mantelpiece. Covering the side tables. There were certificates too, framed and hung between the pictures. Awards for tennis tournaments and music competitions, from what Molly could see. The worst of them all was an enormous gold colored trophy on the coffee table in the middle of the room. A plaque on the base of it read "Hepplewhite Lawn Tennis Club Family Tennis Tournament Award for Playing Tennis".

"This is creepy," said Bella looking around the walls in dismay. "I know humans like to keep pictures of themselves in case they forget what they look like, but this is a bit over the top."

"I know but focus. We haven't time. We've only an hour before they come back. We've got so much to do," said Molly.

CHAPTER THIRTEEN

A Few More Tricks...

Molly dropped her backpack onto the polished coffee table and unzipped it. The box of tricks from Mr. Mountebank's Humbug Emporium went next to the backpack. She carefully unlatched the lid.

"Are we all ready? Right....Winston, here's the itching powder. I'll unscrew the lid for you, so carry it carefully. Don't spill it on you Winston - it'll itch for ages if you do."

"But yet you give it to the dog," said Freya, pausing in a detailed paw washing. "He'll drop it before he's halfway up the stairs. You know how clumsy he is."

"Freya!" said Molly. "There's no need to be mean to him." She turned back to the dog, whose head drooped sadly. "You'll do great, Winston. Just - be careful, that's all. Make sure you pay special attention to their underwear and socks. Check the top two drawers of the dresser in each bedroom, that's where they will probably be."

"Duck, you take the sugar cubes. They'll put these in their morning tea I bet. The sugar pot is the round one with the lid in the middle of the kitchen table. Add these four cubes to the pot and make sure you put the lid back on straight."

"What will they do Molly?" asked Duck, nudging one of the cubes with her beak.

"They turn your tongue green for several hours. It's a Mr. Mountebank special," said Molly. "They don't make you ill or anything, but your tongue looks awful. Make sure you put all four..." But there were now just three sugar cubes on the table, and one guilty looking goat. "Jinks!"

Jinks tried not to crunch the last of the sugar cube in his mouth, but he couldn't resist it. His large tongue flicked out and licked the last of the stray sweet crystals from his lips. His large green tongue.

"Yes, ladies and gentlemen, it turns your tongue exactly that shade of green." Molly rolled her eyes. *That goat! He just can't control himself in the presence of sugar. I should have known.*

"No more, Jinks, or there'll be none for the Hendersons. I'll put the rest in this bag for you to carry, Duck, and make sure you don't lick them. It's going to be hard enough to explain Jinks and his tongue to Grandma." She scooped the remaining sugar cubes into a small paper bag and placed it next to the pot of itching power on the table.

Next, she pulled out a large red tin pot with holes in the lid and placed it next to the bag of sugar cubes.

"For you, Jinks, a very large pepper pot. At least you won't want to eat much of that. We're going to make them sneeze till their noses explode. I want you to shake pepper onto the air vents, into the tissue boxes, and their washcloths. Got that?"

"Air vents, tissue boxes, washcloths," repeated the goat, nodding with enthusiasm to try to make up for his moment of naughtiness. A delicious sugar cube though, and worth getting into trouble for.

"Freya, I need you to go round the house and find a few windows to leave slightly open. Ones that they won't discover tonight. We need to get some cold breezes blowing through. Make sure at least a couple of them are upstairs ones big enough for a Duck to get through. Duck will have a special mission tonight, after dark." Freya merely nodded in agreement and carried on cleaning her right ear.

"Lastly, Bella, I want you to go and find a good place to hide in the kitchen, where you can be heard clearly. You're going to need your best BBC announcer's voice for your trick."

"What about you Molly?" asked Winston. "What will you do?"

Molly grinned and opened the box of tricks again.

"I have here Mr. Mountebank's World-Famous Cushions. One on each of the kitchen chairs should do it I thought. Want to see?" She grabbed one from the box and blew it up as big as it would go. The cushion went on the table.

Molly grabbed Bella and plonked her on top of the cushion. It gave out a loud wobbly fart. Bella squawked and flew up into the air.

"That wasn't me!" she said. "I did not make that noise!" Poor Bella blushed a painful red. She flapped and chattered in embarrassment, running round the tabletop in circles. Jinks bleated at the funny noise and Winston woofed enthusiastically.

Only Freya regarded the scene with disdain. She failed to find such tricks funny. Molly could barely breathe for laughing. But there was no time for messing around. She waved her hands at the others to quieten them all down.

"It's supposed to make that noise Bella. That's what they'll do when a Henderson sits down on them. Do calm down. Now, any questions? No. Good. Go for it, everyone!"

The animals attempted to stand to attention. Various paws and wings and hooves went up in a sloppy salute. Winston pawed the tub of itching powder Molly offered to him and grasped it in between his teeth.

"Careful with that, Winston, you don't want to get it on your fur," warned Molly.

Winston nodded gingerly, turned and headed carefully for the stairs. Jinks bounded up behind him with the large tin pepper pot slung over one of his horns and showing the unbridled enthusiasm any true goat has for a staircase.

"-Atch ou' inks!" growled Winston. The pot held carefully between his teeth made it difficult to talk.

"Sorry, what did you say, Winston?" Jinks pushed past him, nearly spilling the itching powder everywhere. The pepper pot swung back and forth, gently dusting the air with a fine black powder.

As he ran through it, the powder filled his nostrils. Jinks stopped. He reared back on his hind legs and nearly knocked Winston over again.

"-Inks!" mumbled the exasperated Winston. "-Areful!"

Too late - Jinks lost control. An enormous sneeze exploded out of him. He slid backwards down the stairs, bumping down each step in turn. "Ow! Choo! Ow! Choo!" All the way down the stairs, nearly taking Winston and the itching powder down with him.

***

Back in the living room, Duck grabbed the paper bag of sugar cubes from the table and held it in her beak. With a muffled quacking, she headed for the kitchen, followed by Bella in search of a hiding place.

My goodness, what a quacking and banging, thought Molly. She grabbed the rest of the whoopee cushions, the backpack and case full of tricks and followed.

The sky gradually grew darker and darker. A loud crack of thunder made them all jump. Molly looked anxiously out into the garden. As if a switch had been flipped, a torrent of rain fell in sheets, flooding the back garden and filling puddles of mud as she watched.

They'll come straight back in this, Molly thought. She shivered. *Time to speed things up and get out of here.* She set the whoopee cushions on the kitchen chairs at record speed and glanced around the kitchen.

Radio! she thought, *nearly forgot that.* She grabbed the small radio from the windowsill. Fumbling a little with the fiddly back, Molly pulled out the batteries and shoved them into the nearest drawer. *OK, that should be it. Time to go.*

She yelled up the stairs. "All done guys?"

Jinks popped his head out from a room at the end of the landing and nodded. "We're all peppered up Molly. In fact, I ran out of pepper and started using talcum powder as well. Is there anything else we should do up here?"

"No, no time Jinks. We need to get everybody out right now!"

Freya slunk out of the living room to join them. Winston bounded out of Petunia's bedroom, draped in a fluffy pink boa and spitting feathers. "Winston!" said Molly. "Put that back right now. Did you get all of them?"

"Six dresser drawers all dusted, Boss. I even added a little something to the bathroom towels."

"Good thinking. That will drive them crazy. Is everything back as we found it?"

"All shipshape and ready for sea," said the giant dog. "How much time do we have?"

"Not much. It's time to go," said Molly, leading her troops back downstairs and grabbing the backpack and the box of tricks. "Guys, we're leaving now. Will you be okay in the pantry, Bella?"

"I'll be fine, Molly," said Bella. "Now go, before they get back. And don't tell Robbie I'm here. He'll only worry."

"Be careful. Let's go. They'll be back any minute with this rain. Quick, let's go out the back way. We'll have to climb over the fence."

Molly opened the back door and Winston, Duck and Jinks bounded out into the thickly falling rain and splashed their way down to the fence which separated this garden from the farmyard.

Cats and rain! thought Molly, as Freya cowered between her legs. She scooped up the puffed-up bundle, shut the door hard behind them, and ran - juggling a struggling cat, a backpack and the case.

They could barely hear each other over the roar of water hitting the ground. Duck flapped her way over the fence and Molly searched frantically along the sodden wood panels. Her clothes stuck wetly to her, weighing her down and making everything so much more difficult.

"It's here somewhere," she said breathlessly. The others watched her in confusion as she felt along the fence with her fingertips. "It's near the honeysuckle, I'm sure, oh thank goodness." She had found the loose panel just in time and slid it to one side. "Come on everyone!"

They piled through, one at a time, and slammed the panel back into place. Molly leaned against the fence in relief, gasping for breath so hard it hurt her chest.

"I can't wait to see what happens next," yelled Jinks over the pounding rain.

CHAPTER FOURTEEN

The Terrible Lurgy

Night fell and then the sun rose again a few hours later, as it usually does.

There may have been a small excursion by an unnamed duck into the house next door under cover of the aforementioned night. That duck may have been wearing a bright, blue headband and carrying a small paintbrush and a tiny pot of red paint. But it was dark, so we will probably never know…

The air smelt fresh and clean after the previous evening's shower, like laundry flapping on a line. The birds sang happily in the dripping trees. Just regular chirping from the birds, but with background harmonies provided by the chorus of singing sheep and an out of tune llama.

The morning chores were done as usual. Even on

a Monday, perhaps especially on a Monday, the chickens must be fed, Hampton needed grooming and Donald had to be chased out of the vegetable patch. It looked to the outside world like a regular Monday morning in the farmyard. But it felt as though everyone held their breath, waiting for something to happen.

By six o'clock, they had all given up pretending to do anything useful.

By half past six, Molly and most of the animals were sitting behind the front hedge, sneaking regular peeks at the house next door.

"What are they doing in there?" said Winston. "How do people stay in bed so long in the mornings? Don't they have school and work to go to?"

Freya appeared as if by magic, jumped over Winston and landed on top of the fence. The dog growled and snapped at the tip of her tail, which she flicked out of his reach. Freya smirked at his frustration.

"If you ask me, they don't stay in bed long enough," she said. "All this dashing about they all do. It's all highly inefficient. A good nap is the best thing anyone can have. People don't appreciate a good nap enough."

Freya sat herself bolt upright, tail wrapped around her paws and eyes trained on the windows of the next house. She could sit like this for hours if necessary, like a Queen's Guard on duty. Normally she would have curled up in a patch of sunlight and made the most of a quiet Monday morning.

But the wait was too exciting. Even paw washing held no appeal today.

"But we don't want them to nap," chimed in Jinks, his hooves clattering against the fencing. His nose kept edging up above the top of the fence and Molly kept nudging it back down, in case their targets spotted a nosy goat. "We want them up and drinking tea and putting on all their clothes. I want to see what happens. I bet they come screaming out of their house and run down the road and never come back. What an amazing plan!"

"A very good plan," said Molly, tapping his nose down again. "But we need to stay calm, Jinks. If they spot us watching, they're going to guess that something is going on." *And who could fail to spot an over excited goat.*

A loud snore interrupted her. It came from somewhere behind Winston.

"Is Duck OK?" asked Jinks.

"She's fine, she had a bit of a late night that's all. Robbie - can you slow down? You pecked my toes again." The rooster frantically pecked the ground in circles.

"I'm so sorry, Molly. But what if it doesn't work? What if it all goes wrong? What if my Bella gets into trouble? We shouldn't have sent her in there. Oh, what if, what if...."

"Bella will be fine. She's a smart chicken. She's vital to the plan, Robbie." *I hope she's woken up in time,* thought Molly. *She might not have heard Robbie's dawn call from inside the pantry. If she overslept, none of it will work.*

At last, the hands on Molly's watch clicked round to seven o' clock precisely. It was time.

Mrs. Henderson had opened the kitchen window wide, letting the fresh air in and the tantalizing smell of buttered toast out. Molly and the animals could see her moving around and humming loudly.

The clock on the radio struck the seventh chime. A voice started speaking. A rich, plummy voice. Belonging to someone who was born with not just a silver spoon in their mouth, as it were, but a whole cutlery tray full.

"On the news today...." It was a distinctly posher accent than the one Mrs. Henderson usually attempted, and certainly better bred than Tracy who normally read the morning news.

"Who's that?" asked Mrs. Henderson, looking frantically around her.

"It's the radio Mum, don't be daft," said Petunia, entering the kitchen and scraping back one of the chairs.

"Hmmm hmmm. As I was saying..." continued the voice.

Petunia sat down heavily on the chair. A huge Brrrrrrtttt! erupted from beneath her.

"Petunia - manners!" her mother said. Her eyes widened in surprise. "But..."

"Excuse me," the mysterious voice continued. Mrs. Henderson stared at the radio with a slightly raised eyebrow.

"BBC reports are in of a mysterious illness sweeping the suburbs of the city. Apparently, there is a serious sickness going round which starts with coughing, sneezing, and very loud farting. Patients then start to become terminally itchy, and the final stage is a strong green tinge to the tongue. The mysterious illness has been dubbed the Terrible Lurgy by scientists, who say they have never seen anything like it, but that it has mostly been carried and spread by The Common People. That is all" The hidden Bella finished her announcement with a loud click, as if the radio were being switched off.

"That doesn't sound very polite," said Mrs. Henderson haughtily. "Sneezing and itching and nasty noises. We shan't be having any of that around here, thank you very much. Fortunately, it is h'only for Common People, and h'we are too well bred for that." Mrs. Henderson always pronounced several more H's than actually existed in her sentences. She thought it showed everybody exactly how posh she was, which was obviously posher than everybody else.

Petunia shifted in her seat, trying to get comfortable. Another loud blart rang out from beneath her.

"Petunia!" said her mother sharply. "H'I will not tell you again."

"But I didn't do it," said the puzzled Petunia. She looked under her chair, then under the table, but could not see where the embarrassing sound came from. "I wouldn't mind having a green tongue," she said.

"The lady on the news said you could get a green tongue. That would be fun, that would make them laugh at school. I bet Miss Goody Two shoes

Jessica Blunt doesn't have a green tongue. All my friends would envy me if I had a green tongue."

"What friends? You don't have any friends," teased her brother as he burst through the kitchen door, his hair still dripping wet from a shower. He shook out the fluffy blue towel he carried and started to rub it vigorously over his head.

"Alastair, I've told you before, don't do that in here. It's not...Not... Aaahhh, aaaaahhhh, aaaaaaahh - CHOOOOOOOOO!" A most unladylike sneeze erupted from Mrs. Henderson as the pepper coating the towel escaped into the air. "ACCCHHOOOOOO!" She sneezed again, and again, until the tears were streaming down her cheeks.

Alastair and Petunia stared at their mother. Her usual sneezes sounded more like a genteel poodle barking delicately for attention. They had never before heard her make a noise like that. Alastair slowly lowered the towel, and the pepper laden towel began to work its magic on him. He felt the tickle in his nose begin to build.

"Oh no, I'm going to..." A giant sneeze made him rock back on his heels. "Ow!"

"What is going on down there?" bellowed Mr. Henderson from the bedroom upstairs.

"Sit down, Alastair, before your father comes down. Stop messing about with that towel, I don't know where..." another sneezing fit overtook Mrs. Henderson and she leaned against the sink helplessly.

Slightly confused, Alastair sat as he was told. As

he did, another loud farting noise ripped the air. Petunia smirked as her mother glared at her son. "I don't know what you two are playing at..." she started, before another explosive sneeze stopped her.

"Pass the sugar." Petunia slid the sugar bowl across the table to her brother, who promptly added the top three cubes to his waiting mug of tea and stirred it enthusiastically. He picked up the mug and slurped down a large mouthful of the steaming tea.

"It's hot," said Petunia automatically.

"Arrrgh!" whimpered Alastair and started trying to blow on his tongue to cool it down. His green tongue. Petunia stared at the lizard looking tongue sticking out his mouth.

"It's green!" she screamed. "You've got the green tongue - I wanted the green tongue. It's not fair - you always get everything first!" She stood up and stamped her foot, her fists clenching and unclenching as she watched her brother trying to look at his own tongue.

The door slammed open and Mr. Henderson strode into the kitchen.

"What is all this racket?" he roared. "I'm already late. I'll take that." He grabbed the offending mug of tea from Alastair's hand and poured the remainder of the scalding liquid down in one go.

"Aaarrrggh! It's hot!" he yelled. Then sneezed. Then he started to scratch.

"Your face!" Mrs. Henderson's nostrils pinched and her eyebrows knitted together as she looked at her husband.

"You're covered in spots. And your tongue is bright green. No. It can't be. On the news a minute ago. It's the Terrible Lurgy. We've caught the Terrible Lurgy. But it's for Common People. It said so. We can't have something for Common People." She sneezed again, spraying globulous green snot across the room. Mr. Henderson reared back in horror.

The final indignity began. First, behind Petunia's neck, then below Alastair's left ankle. Mr. Henderson felt it niggling his magnificent beard, and Mrs. Henderson's elbows all started at about the same time. Just a little tickle at first. Then a vaguely annoying irritation. Finally, a full blown, make your teeth clench kind of itch which spread from one part of the body to all the rest. The itching powder was doing its job, with spectacular results.

Molly, Jinks and the others jumped as the back door crashed open and Mr. Henderson staggered out first, leaping and flinging his arms around like an angry gorilla. He bellowed loudly enough to wake the whole street and faces began to appear at doors and windows with unusual speed. Small red spots covered his nose and forehead, and his tongue glowed a bright, unnatural green.

Mr. Henderson barely noticed that the whole street was watching him. He scratched and jumped around and shouted fit to burst. He pulled at his hair. He tugged at his enormous beard. He went magnificently red in the face.

Mrs. Henderson came leaping out of the front door behind him, sneezing explosively and screaming between each huge sneeze.

"Somebody call an.... ATCHOOOOOOOO! An ambulance.... Now! ATCHOOOO!" she shrieked.

"It's not fair! His tongue is GREEN! If anyone should have a green tongue, it should be me. You always let him have everything first!" yelled Petunia at her parents. She clung to the door frame and tried to scratch up against it with her back. Then she threw herself on the gravel path and rolled back and forth.

The adult Hendersons jumped and hollered and scratched and yelled. They crashed into each other and the patio furniture. Mr. Henderson jumped over the moaning Petunia. Mrs. Henderson fell backwards into the ornamental pond, surprising the resident frog. She screamed.

Molly could hold it no longer. She howled with laughter. The animals joined in, honking, bleating and woofing happily.

Nobody noticed Alastair quietly opening the door for a chicken. He took a quick look at his family and bent down to say something to Bella. She snuck out speedily with a couple of whoopee cushions tucked under one wing and headed straight for the garden gate.

"Oh Jinks!" said Molly, "It was a wonderful idea. Look at them!" But she realized too late how much noise they were making.

Mr. Henderson spotted Molly and the others hiding behind the hedge. He heard the laughter.

He knew they must have had something to do with it. He didn't know what. But that didn't stop him.

Mr. Henderson stormed over to the hedge and reached over to grab hold of Molly's arm. His spotty, wobbling face blazed scarlet all over, apart from the green tongue and the bristling beard, but he didn't look nearly as funny at close range.

"You!" he spat at her. "It's all your fault. You and that grandmother of yours. Your animals have made us ILL! Do you see this? Spots and green tongues and sneezing and itching. This is all down to your animals. I'm calling Mr. Bennet this morning. I'll tell that Inspector to have you gone by the end of this week! All of you!" He let go of Molly's arm and shook his fist at the group of animals. None of them were laughing or smiling any longer.

He turned and stormed back into his house, pushing his family ahead of him. "End of the week!" he yelled before the door slammed shut behind them.

"Maybe that didn't go so well after all," said Molly. "What on earth are we going to do now?"

CHAPTER FIFTEEN

The Second Plan

The first plan might not have worked on the Hendersons, but it wasn't long before the animals started coming up with new ideas to deal with them. Not all of these ideas were sensible. *They very rarely are*, thought Molly.

"Let's breed giant chickens to peck their houses down!"

"We should put alligators in their garden pond."

"Oooh - yes, we could ask Morris."

"Why don't we create a green slime which will ooze out of their toilets and baths and cover the carpets?"

"Or an invasion of aliens could come and plant turnips all over their garden." Donald offered this last idea. He had a preference for turnips and thought there were never enough of them to be found.

"I have it, Molly, I have a plan," said Hampton, swishing his tail and flicking his mane in excitement. "People don't like spooky things do they? Not like horses, we don't get scared of things ever." Jinks snorted at this. He had seen Hampton bolt across the yard when a squirrel had landed on his back before.

"We horses have fought on battlefields you know, young Private. We are scared of nothing. But some people, on the other hand, are terrified of things that go bump in the night, aren't they?"

"It can happen," said Molly. "Why? What are you thinking?" *Are we talking about a pet vampire? Or maybe hiring a scary clown? At least the animals' ideas are never predictable.*

"What if their house was filled with ghosts? Then they would leave lickety-split. They would march right out of there. We need to convince them that the house is haunted." He nodded along and pawed at the ground as he spoke, pleased with his plan.

Molly stroked her braids. "But their house has never been haunted before. Why would ghosts suddenly move in this week?"

"Hampton may have something there," said the rooster beside her. Robbie was still annoyed that he had missed out on the glory of the expedition to the Henderson house. He desperately wanted to be involved in the next mission. "Ghosts would scare them out of there. Then they won't come bothering us. I think we should talk some ghosts into moving in next door."

"Do you know any ghosts, Robbie?"

"Well, no. But I bet Jinks does. He knows everybody."

While it was true that Jinks was a very friendly goat who did know a lot of strange characters, no ghosts were listed in his address book. But it had sparked an idea in Molly's head.

Ghosts? Hmmm... Perhaps the appearance of some ghosts.

"Right, everyone. I need paper, a pencil, some crayons and a large bag of toffees to figure this out. I'm going down to the Grotto to work on it. Don't disturb me unless it's an emergency!"

Molly grabbed the essentials and settled herself in the old wooden chair under the oak tree. The animals watched from around the farmyard, but they knew when Molly needed some space.

Every so often, a page would float gently over the back of the chair and land on the grass behind her. The discarded papers and toffee wrappers gradually piled up, but no one dared disturb her. Molly hunched over her drawings, muttering and frowning. One particularly annoying diagram had her scrunching up the sheet of paper and hurling it over her left shoulder, where it boinked Duck on the beak.

With a quack, Duck picked it up and took the balled-up paper to the others.

"Here, flatten it out. Look, use your paw to hold that corner."

"What's this line here?" said Jinks, pointing at a squiggle with a delicate hoof.

"Is it a porcupine? Or maybe a mouse. Why would she draw a mouse?" said Bella. She pecked around the paper, but it made no more sense with holes in it than it had before.

"No, I think it is a pulley," said Freya. She had a typical cat's talent for understanding mechanical things. Bolts and gate locks and things like that were never safe from her. But she wasn't able to work it out any more than the other animals could. She turned the paper back and forth, then twisted her head around to see if it made any more sense that way up. It didn't.

By lunchtime, most of them had lost interest and wandered off to argue about hats and elephants and other important things. Freya and Duck made their way to the wooden chair and crept up close to Molly's legs. Another sheet of paper flew away over the back of the chair. A toffee wrapper joined it.

"Molly," Duck started hesitantly, "Freya has an idea."

Freya sat back on her haunches and began to slowly wash herself. Molly finally looked up from her scribbling and gradually her gaze focused on the cat.

"Go on," she tried to say, through a mouthful of sticky toffee.

"In my younger days," Freya began, "before I found my way to the Flabbergast Farm, you may recall that I grew up as a theater cat. No luckier cat in the business. For me and for them. Black cats bring good luck in the theater you know. And good luck brings cream and sardines for a good cat."

Molly nodded slightly and wrinkled her nose at Freya. "Is there a point to this story? I have two hours to come up with a great plan, and right now, I'm completely stuck."

"That's the toffee," said Duck.

"Oh, there is, my dear, there is most certainly a point. If I may continue..." Freya sprang effortlessly onto the arm of the chair and stuck her nose in the air. "But if you are too busy to listen, I quite understand."

There are few things so easily offended in this world as a cat. Perfectly aware of this, Molly wobbled between making Freya happy or coming up with a brilliant idea. However, Freya had a tendency to sleep on Molly's head if anyone upset her, which was mildly uncomfortable to say the least. So Molly gave in and tried to not look too impatient.

"No, of course I'm never too busy for you Freya. But I would love it if it's something to do with ghosts."

"Actually, it is. One summer season we were putting on a production of the Scottish play."

"Do you mean Macbeth?" asked Duck, her head tilted to one side. "I loved the sword fighting in that one. They were filming it in the studio next door one time."

"Shhhhhhh...," said Freya. "You should never say the name of that play. It's bad luck."

"Sorry, sorry, sorry, sorry," quacked Duck.

"But yes, that Scottish play. And there's a scene

where this ghost turns up to scare Mac....I mean, the new Scottish King. My friend, the Stage Manager, had this really clever trick to fool all the people in the audience into thinking they were seeing a real ghost on stage."

"How on earth did he do that?" said Molly, fascinated by the story.

"He used a stage trick called Pepper's Ghost. He had the actor playing the ghost walking up and down underneath the stage and then he had this huge piece of glass hung at an angle facing the stage. When he pointed a big light at the ghost, it would bounce the image up onto the stage. You could see it and see through it at the same time. It really did look like a ghost. It spooked me the first time I saw it, and I'm not easily scared."

"Wow!" said Molly and Duck.

"That sounds perfect for our plan. How do you think we could do that at the Henderson house?"

Freya put one paw on the top of the wooden chair and stood herself up as tall as possible, then jumped lightly to the top of the chair. "Still too low," she muttered, then climbed on top of Molly's head. "Keep still girl. I'm trying to estimate the angle. It's no good, I need to get higher."

"Use the tree, use the tree," sang Duck, rearing up and flapping her wings.

Freya nodded and in three short strides and a huge leap reached the lowest branch of the old oak tree. She squinted over the fence into the back of the neighbors' house. Tilting her head on one side, then the other, she wriggled her nose twice and twitched her whiskers three times.

"I think, if we opened the sunroom door to exactly the right angle and had an actor by the fence here, and a light up there..." She lapsed into silence as she worked out the details.

"Yes!" she said eventually. "That would work. We just need a pretend ghost."

"Would a Jinks do?" suggested Molly.

"I think a Jinks would be perfect," said Freya. "Now what else can we do to scare the Hendersons?"

CHAPTER SIXTEEN

A New Ally

Molly, Freya and Duck put their heads together and huddled over the scribbles on Molly's last sheet of paper.

There was a loud crash from the other side of the fence. Molly slid off the chair in surprise. The chair tipped backwards, and Freya fell, gracefully, to the floor.

"Who's there?" said Molly loudly, trying to shove all the pieces of paper under Duck to hide their plans. "What do you want?"

The bush on the other side of the fence rustled again and a face popped up in the middle of it, a little scratched and flustered, underneath a cloud of ginger hair.

"Alastair?" said Molly. She grabbed the chair arm and pulled herself up from the cold ground, shielding Duck and her stash of incriminating plans.

"What do you want?" she asked.

"Well, that's nice," said Alastair. "I only wondered what you were up to."

"Nothing." Even Molly could tell that she didn't sound convincing. "Just hanging out."

"Right. Nice fairy thing by the way. I thought those were for little kids."

"Why are you so interested in it then?" Molly was starting to get impatient. "Did you want something? Only, we're busy."

"Yeah, looks like it." Alastair shrugged his shoulders and started to back away from the fence, but the hedge was making it a little difficult. "Ow!" One branch snagged his t-shirt, and a twig poked him in the eye. "Oof!"

"Serves you right for spying on people," said Molly, with a smirk.

"I wasn't... well, alright. Maybe a bit. I just wanted to see...." Alastair didn't seem to know what he wanted to see. "The green tongue business, and the spots, and the itching. That was something to do with you, wasn't it?"

Molly glanced at Freya. The cat was watching Alastair through slitted eyes. The tip of her tail flicked a warning not to say too much. Molly said nothing.

"Only, I saw the chicken and the whoopee cushions," Alastair went on. He tried to untangle his left arm from the particularly unfriendly twig, but the hedge was having none of it. "I let it out of the kitchen. The chicken I mean, not the whoopee cushions. It got stuck in the kitchen. Why was there a chicken in our kitchen when all that was going on?"

I don't know what to make of you, thought Molly. *On the one hand, you're a Henderson. All Hendersons are, obviously, mean and evil and not to be trusted in any way. On the other hand, you always look like don't want to be there whenever I see you with your family.* Right now, he was definitely looking more puzzled than angry. *Pale as well. Washed out and chubby. Never done any real work in his life. Still, if he saw Bella and let her out...perhaps he isn't all bad.*

"You saw Bella?" she asked quietly.

"Is that the chicken?"

"Yeah. Bella. She's a she, not an it, thank you."

"OK, she. I don't know much about animals to be honest. Why was she in the kitchen?" His brow wrinkled as he thought about it.

"Aren't you mad about the green tongue?"

"Mad?" He laughed. "I thought that was really funny actually. The itching powder, not so much. But the farting and the tongues and the spots, those were so funny. Seeing my dad leaping round the garden, and Petunia rolling around on the floor, that was hysterical. I had to listen to my Mum complain for hours afterwards, but it was worth it. I figured it must be some sort of trick, but I couldn't work out how or why at first. Or who, until I saw the chicken. Bella," he corrected himself.

"Why?" said Molly. "Surely you know why?"

"Well, I know my parents are kind of bossy to everyone in the street, but I didn't know you hated us that much," said Alastair, looking away from her.

"They've made a complaint to Mr. Bennet, the Health Inspector, about our animals. We're getting evicted at the end of the week because of your parents." Tears filled Molly's eyes. She clenched her fists tight until the nails pinched her palms and took a deep breath. *Don't show it. Don't let him see.*

Alastair's mouth fell open. "They did that? They tried to get you kicked out?"

Molly sniffed. "Not just tried. Pretty much succeeded. We're trying to scare them away before we get kicked out. It didn't work though. Your dad figured out it was us. He's even angrier now."

"I'm really sorry. I have no idea why they're like this. I hate living with them; they're so mean to everybody." Alastair's shoulders slumped. "Everybody hates us. Even at the tennis club."

"I think your farm is pretty cool," he said. "The goat is insane though," he added. "I'm sure I saw it eating a hat the other day."

"That's Jinks," said Molly. "Fair description. He does like a good hat."

There was a long pause. Not the type where everyone has run out of things to say but are happy to sit together in the silence, or the sort where glares across the battle lines are working up to somebody getting hit. This was more of a 'nobody knows what happens next' sort of quiet. Alastair broke it.

"Is there anything I can do to help?" he asked.

Molly and Freya and Duck looked at each other for a long moment.

"I think we can trust him," said Freya eventually.

Alastair looked at Molly, then Duck, then stared at Freya. His jaw dropped again, and his eyes opened wide. Then he shook himself free of the over affectionate hedge and laughed loudly.

"You had me going there for a minute. I thought your cat was talking to me."

"Hmm. Really? She's a cat." Molly glared at Freya.

"Don't worry - I won't tell anyone." Alastair tried to close one eye in an exaggerated wink, and nearly stabbed himself on a wayward twig.

"No one would believe you anyway. They'd think you were going crazy. Half the street thinks that anyway." Molly grinned at the memory of the Hendersons leaping round their garden.

Alastair smiled back. "That was a pretty awesome stunt you pulled. Where did you get those sugar cubes? And the radio trick - how did you manage that? What are you going to do next? What can I do?" The questions poured out of Alastair. It was the most excited Molly had ever seen him.

"We need to get back in your house when your family are all out."

"You'll definitely need my help then. My dad took the spare key away - he figured you probably used that to get in. But I can leave a window unlocked or something. C'mon, what's the plan? When are we going to do it?"

"It needs to be soon. We have to get reinspected before the end of Friday or Mr. Bennet will kick us out."

"Wednesday then. We always have to go and play tennis on Wednesday evenings. You can get in then and set stuff up."

"That works." Molly paused. "We thought we could make a ghost appear."

Alastair's eyes widened. "Whoooo. That would be brilliant. They would be terrified. They really believe in all that stuff, especially my dad. What else?"

Molly shook her head. "That was it so far. You got any bright ideas?"

Alastair tapped the top of the fence with his free hand and pursed his lips. His eyes narrowed as he thought. "Actually, yes." He wriggled free of the hedge at last and pulled himself up. "Can you give me a hand? I might have an idea or two. Do you have some paper and a pen?"

"Wait, wait," said Molly. "You'll hurt yourself. There's the loose fence panel down here, by the tree. If we slide it, you can get through here."

"I had no idea this was here. Wow, it's a tight squeeze, but..." After a couple of minutes of huffing and puffing and scraping through, Alastair stood inside the farmyard. "Oh, this is amazing. You've got sheep and a chicken house and a barn and is that a llama?" His chestnut-colored eyes widened as he tried to take in everything around him.

"Well, it is a farmyard," said Molly. "What were you expecting?"

"I know, but... this is great. You can't move. I won't let my parents get you kicked out. We have to find a way to stop them. I think the ghost idea is good, but we have to make it really scary."

"We know that," said Molly sharply. She waved the well scribbled on piece of paper under Alastair's nose. "What do you think we've been working on all afternoon?"

"We? Do you mean you and the cat? Can it draw too? Or was that the duck?" He laughed wildly.

"Molly does all the drawing," said Freya smoothly. "Opposable thumbs and all that. But she's not the only one who can come up with ideas."

Alastair jumped and stared at her. His mouth opened slackly and his eyes bugged out at the smug looking cat. "You... you ... you really can talk?"

"Have we not already gone through this?" Freya yawned and started washing one of her front paws delicately.

"Yes, but... but... I thought it was a trick. I thought it must have been Molly talking. You know, like a ventrilililoloquist type fella. You really can?"

Freya just rolled her eyes at him in reply and started on the next paw.

"Yes, she really can," said Molly. "Can we move on now? Only we don't have a lot of time to figure out the rest of our brilliant plan. You'd better have some good ideas to make us glad we've let you in on it. And you'd better not tell anyone about Freya. Even your sister."

"Petunia? She's the last person I would tell anything to. She'd try and steal your cat and use her to win the school talent show. No, you can trust me. Not a peep. Wow, a talking cat. Really a talking cat. That's awesome. Not a word, I promise." So saying, Alastair ran a finger along his skinny lips, as if zipping them shut.

Reluctantly, Molly held out the piece of paper to him again. "Here, have you heard of Pepper's ghost? It's a classic theater trick," she said with confidence, as if she hadn't just discovered it herself.

"Pepper's ghost? No, that's a new one on me. How does that work?"

Molly and Alastair sat down with a cat and a duck to talk, eat the bag of toffees and save the Flabbergast Farm.

By the time the sun sank between the trees, they had their new plan and a very big pile of toffee wrappers scattered all around the fairy grotto.

CHAPTER SEVENTEEN

Telling the Animals

The whole family of animals gathered round the fire pit by the house to wait for her. The darkness crept closer and the flames flickered brightly as they chattered nervously. The animals huddled together as they waited nervously to hear Molly's plan.

"Do you think she knows where we can get a ghost?" asked Larry the llama in a worried voice.

"How do we know a ghost would be on our side?" said a clucky sounding voice. "Some ghosts are mean, perhaps it would be on their side and then it would come and haunt us! I don't think Molly has thought this through." Bella flapped her wings nervously and scratched at the floor.

Jinks pawed the ground next to her. "How many ghosts would we need to scare away the Hendersons? I bet it would be a lot."

"Not real ghosts, sillies." Molly's voice broke through the muttering. The animals moved apart to make a path for her to the fire pit. She threw another couple of logs on the fire and poked it until the flames grew higher and warmer.

She made herself comfortable as close as she could to the flames, spreading an old blanket over her knees and drawing in the smoky plumes in deep, contented breaths. The smell of a real fire always whispered hints of distant memories. In the stillness of the moment, Molly let go of her worries and watched the flickers of light play across the faces of her friends.

"Just pretend ghosts," Freya said. "Pepper's ghost. It's an old theater trick to make ghosts appear on stage." She nudged in to sit beside Molly, her green eyes glowing even more brightly in the red light. The animals settled back down, hoping to hear more.

"Who is Pepper?" asked Lavender. "Why does he have his own ghost?"

"Can we borrow his ghost?" said Donald.

"Forget Pepper for a moment." Molly hushed them with her hands. Really, trying to keep their attention was a job by itself.

"There's something else you should know. Alastair knows that we played those tricks on them."

"Who is Alastair?" asked Lavender. "Is he friends with Pepper?"

"No, no, no. He's the Henderson boy."

A gasp went up from all the animals. They

glanced nervously over at the neighbors" house and then back to Molly.

"And he knows that Freya can talk."

Another sharp intake of air from most of the animals. Only Freya and Duck looked unconcerned.

"But how, Molly? How did he find out?" Jinks said what they were all thinking. "Does everybody know now?"

"Not at all," said Molly, trying to sound reassuring. "Freya spoke to him."

"Assume you have your reasons, Miss Freya," said Hampton, shaking his mane as he spoke. "Not clear what they are, but sure you know what you're doing."

"Actually, I think she was right. He had a few helpful ideas. You remember how they love to watch those scary horror movies and you can hear the screams from the end of the road?" Heads nodded nervously and hooves pawed the ground. The noises from next door had scared some of them the first few times.

"You've seen their nasty decorations all over the front of the house at Halloween?" More nodding and pawing. "We're going to use that against them. They believe in all that sort of stuff, ghosties and ghoulies and things like that. We'll make the ghosties and ghoulies come to life at number 14. We're going to get some help from Alastair to do that."

"But how?" Jinks asked. "It sounds pretty scary."

"For them, not for us," said Duck. "We'll scare

them so badly that it will be them leaving at the end of the week, not us." She went into stance number 17, - The Dragonfly - legs apart and wings crossed in front of her and glared straight ahead. "It's time to fight back, friends." The other animals cheered and clapped.

"Hmm." Molly tried not to roll her eyes at Duck's theatrics. "Ladies and gentlemen..." Molly stood up suddenly and crossed to a big flat patch of dry dirt behind Jinks. She looked for a sturdy stick and started scratching a crude picture with it into the sandy earth. As she poked at it, a series of squares and circles and arrows started to appear.

"Now, pay attention, because you all have a job to do...."

CHAPTER EIGHTEEN

Anyone for Tennis?

"Do we all have our tennis rackets?" called Mrs. Henderson as they piled out of the house on Wednesday evening. Mr. Henderson, Mrs. Henderson, Alastair and Petunia were all dressed in sparkling bright tennis whites and carried a matching racket in their right hands. The street echoed emptily, but the occasional net curtain twitched as they stepped out and formed an orderly line on the driveway.

"All present and correct," said Mr. Henderson, shaking his racket with enthusiasm. His shorts were a little too short, his shirt slightly too bright, and they both had knife sharp creases ironed into them. Mr. Henderson crackled as he moved; clouds of starch flew off his tennis whites with every stride.

"Mine is here," said Alastair, gloomily waving his racket in the air. He hated Wednesday tennis. The tight white shorts which showed off his chunky legs and knobbly knees. The pointless running around on a court. The ridiculous showing off to all the other tennis club players. Alastair loathed every minute of it. This Wednesday was even worse, if that was possible. His new friends would be having a blast setting up a load of tricks without him.

"Got mine," said Petunia. She flicked her long black ponytail from side to side and smoothed down the thick fringe which sat squarely across her bushy eyebrows.

"What a wonderful day for tennis," announced Mrs. Henderson. She looked doubtfully at the gathering gray clouds above. "I believe the storm h'is scheduled to hold off until h'at least dark. I do hope so. The Hepplewhite Lawn Tennis Club h'always looks magnificent h'against the sunset in the background. Such h'a picturesque setting for Sunday dinner my dears," she beamed. Her extra H's always appeared extra often on Wednesday afternoons, as soon as the Tennis Club was mentioned.

The Henderson family were incredibly proud of their membership of the HLTC (the Hepplewhite Lawn Tennis Club, in case you weren't paying attention.) They would mention it at every social gathering, in an attempt to impress those who usually didn't even play tennis. It was one of those sorts of clubs where you could join by paying pots of money and then pretending it was because you were better than everybody else.

The only one of them who was mortified by the whole business was Alastair. He hated the clothes, the showing off, the leaping across a court after a stupid little ball. The whole thing was a giant embarrassment to him, but the rest of his family didn't care.

Three of them flashed matching sets of bright white teeth and clasped their tennis rackets enthusiastically as they climbed into the large SUV which filled their driveway. Alastair groaned, flicked a quick glance back at the farmyard, and climbed reluctantly into the back seat. The huge vehicle grunted into life, and they pulled out of the driveway and away down the road. The net curtains twitched once or twice more and then fell still.

***

Jinks ducked back down behind their own hedge, which is quite hard for a goat to do. He galloped back to the other animals who were gathered at the other end of the farmyard. A higgeldy piggeldy pile of crates leaned against the fence next to the Hendersons" garden. A ramp ran to the top of this stack and a rope had been slung over the lowest branch of the old oak tree above it. Molly and the animals had been busy while they were waiting.

"They're clear, Molly," said Jinks, "Let's do it!"

Molly nodded grimly and pressed go on the stopwatch. She hung it over one of the fence posts, and Hampton stationed himself next to it. Too big to get into the neighbor's garden, Hampton had been assigned the important job of timekeeper. Two hours were barely long enough to do everything they needed to. Taking too long would be a disaster. Not only would the Hendersons be back from the HLTC, but Grandma and Daisy would be heading back from the television studios as soon as they'd finished filming the toothpaste commercial.

Duck and a couple of geese had one end of the rope in their beaks and with a great squawking and flapping, they rose in a group above the fence then over into the next-door garden. A large plank of wood hung from the other end of the rope, and it wobbled up to the top of the fence as they lined it up with the first ramp.

"There, Duck, drop the plank there. That's it," said Molly, as one end dropped with a smack into the perfectly trimmed grass on the other side. "Careful now," she continued, as the geese nudged the other end up into position at the top of the fence. Molly grabbed one of their ropes and Jinks the other and they backed up, pulling the plank tight to the fence and then tying it off to the tree behind them. "That should do it," said Molly.

Molly grasped the handles of the battered red wheelbarrow and wheeled it precariously up the ramp to the top of the fence. It was too wide to fit through the gap in the fence, so Jinks had suggested this makeshift ramp. The wheelbarrow lurched to one side and then the other, but eventually Molly reached the top and let out a huge sigh of relief.

"Are we ready?" asked Molly. An assortment of neighs, barks, woofs, whistles and cackles answered her. "Let's go!"

The wheelbarrow was piled high with coils of rope, slithery thin black cables, mysterious little black boxes and all sorts of mysterious gadgets. Molly giggled as she launched herself down the second ramp into the forbidden realm of number 14 and flew across the perfectly trimmed grass.

But she couldn't stop. "Aaaaahhhhh! Help - where are the brakes?" yelled Molly as she tore right through Mr. Henderson's beloved vegetable patch at the bottom of the garden. Lettuces flew up behind her and tomato plants dropped their ripe fruit onto the dirt in disgust. She left a trail of torn leaves and a furrow in the soil with a clear imprint of the wheelbarrow's wheel. "Oops." She heard a clatter of hooves on wood and then a goat landed on her head.

"Jinks - you smell like a compost heap," complained Molly, scrabbling to get out from a pile of wheelbarrow, cables and stinky goat.

"Yes, well, there's a reason for that," said the goat with a huge grin.

"Eurrgh - get off me silly." Molly grabbed one of the goat's horns and used it to pull herself up, slipping and sliding her way to a standing position. She groaned at the sight of the upturned wheelbarrow and the scattered contents. "We don't have time for this. Quick - grab the cables, and Duck, can you pick up the speakers? Oh Freya, thank goodness...."

"We've got one hour and forty-eight minutes, Molly," said Hampton from the other side of the fence. "No time to mess around everyone. They'll be back at a quarter past eight precisely. They always are."

Molly pointed and gave instructions until they had picked everything up again. "Come on, quickly. We must get that big rock up there - geese, you help Duck with that. Winston, I need you to hook these strings of lights across there. Careful with the speakers, we can't break them. I'll check the fence panel; we'll have to get through here later. This bag needs to go up too, Duck...." The list was endless.

"OK, we can do this," said Molly, trying to convince herself as well as the animals. They dashed from one job to another, heaving, shoving, lifting. Molly tugged nervously at her braids and tried to remember everything on their list.

Freya jumped down smoothly into the garden, avoiding the plowed-up vegetable patch and headed over to the sunroom at the end of the house and started pacing up and down by the door. She kept looking towards a point near the fence and then back to the glass door, squinting her eyes almost closed.

"Hurry up, everybody," said Hampton loudly. "It's after eight o'clock." He nudged the large clock Molly had set next to him.

Duck landed with a splat at Molly's side. "The rock is in position, and I think the light string is good. What on earth is Freya up to?"

"She's calculating the position the sunroom door will need to be in. For the Pepper's ghost trick."

"That sounds difficult. Can't she open the door and see?"

"It's locked. Alastair said he'll make sure it's unlocked tonight. He didn't want them to figure out something was going on. But we won't have time to figure out the angle tonight. Freya is working it out now."

"Five minutes, Molly. The wheelbarrow needs to come back over the fence now. Come on everybody. Jinks give Molly a hand, will you?"

Molly had the wheelbarrow lined up at the bottom of the ramp. Without warning, Jinks shoved her hard. Molly and the red wheelbarrow went flying up the plank of wood - so much faster this time without the load. She yelped with surprise and barely kept the wheel on the wood, but within seconds they were up and safely on the other side, landing in an undignified heap in their own farmyard. Jinks rattled up the plank after her, then Duck flew over with the geese, carrying the plank back into the farmyard. As if they had never trespassed into the neighbor's garden, provided nobody looked too carefully at the vegetable patch.

"Two minutes, Molly. We need everybody out now!" bellowed Hampton.

Molly scrambled up on to the fence to try and look over it. Duck perched on the fence post next to her. One job remained unfinished, but it was the most important one. As they watched, Freya extended a paw, sprung out a razor-sharp claw and, lining up invisible measurements, drew a large cross in the soil. Satisfied, she padded back to the fence and hopped up and over in one effortless move, managing to soften her fall by landing on Winston's head before jumping safely to the ground.

"Well, I hope she knows what she's doing," said Duck. "It sounds like that's going to be the most convincing part of our whole plan. I hate to think what will happen if it doesn't work."

"I'm sure she does," said Molly, but Duck heard the slight tremble in her voice.

Not a minute too soon. The familiar roar of the Hendersons" SUV filled the evening air of Chestnut Crescent.

CHAPTER NINETEEN

Night Falls...

The sun set and the moon glowed gently over the suspiciously silent farmyard. The short hand on the grandfather clock in the hall edged towards eleven. Mrs. Flabbergast had already packed herself off to bed with a nice cup of steaming hot cocoa and a toasty hot water bottle. The sounds of teeth brushing, duvet rearranging and book rustling filtered down through the house to the kitchen. Molly and the members of her hand-picked team sat around the table, listening and waiting.

"Did you hear that?" asked Jinks, as two loud clunks came from above, one after another. He tried not to clatter his hoofs on the kitchen tiles as he backed up to the kitchen stove nervously, but every sound echoed through the darkness. The goat tipped his nose upwards as if he could sniff out the source of the clunking.

"Slippers," said Molly, her head tipped to one side. Their voices were low. *But Grandma's hearing is pretty sharp. I know she'd disapprove of us scaring the Hendersons like this. But it has to be done. We just can't let her hear us.*

Molly held a finger to her lips to shush the talkative Jinks. The goat was shivering with the excitement of it all and nothing would keep him quiet for long. There was a slow, loud creak from the room above. Jinks jumped several inches clear of the floor.

"Bedsprings," said Molly.

She had crept back downstairs as soon as her grandmother had checked on her and kissed her cheek. Within ten minutes the old lady would be asleep, the foamy hot chocolate largely undrunk and the book slipping from her fingers to the floor. After that, nothing would disturb her till Robbie the Rooster crowed at the split of dawn.

Ten more minutes. Ten agonizingly long minutes with a twitchy goat, a nervous chicken, a duck quacking under her breath and a big hairy Winston pacing back and forth from the door to the large kitchen window. The only calm creature here, thought Molly, was the curled-up cat on top of the refrigerator.

Freya had settled up there as soon as her dinner and post dinner wash were finished. In Freya's opinion, nothing interesting had happened yet so she would sleep until it did. Molly wished she could do the same, but that was a talent peculiar to cats.

A loud rumbling filled the silence. Then a pause. Another gentle roar reverberated from above.

Molly let go of the breath she didn't realize she had been holding. "Snoring." She crept soundlessly over to the kitchen window and stared out into the darkness. One chance to save their farmyard and all the animals. It all depended upon her. A shiver rattled down her spine.

"Are we doing the right thing?" Molly asked. Her voice barely registered above a whisper, but the animals all had sharp hearing. "I don't want to get my grandmother in more trouble. It's bad enough as it is. What if we get caught and Mr. Bennet blames her and then she loses her animal license completely..." She tailed off, the idea too terrible to contemplate. "What if they really make us leave?" she said very quietly.

"We have to do something," said Winston. "We can't sit and do nothing."

"Things are bad, things are bad," said Bella, strutting around in tight circles. "Things are so bad."

"But what if they figure out it was us?" Molly worried.

"The dog, for once, is right," said the voice from above her head. Molly turned to see Freya stretching slowly on her perch and unfolding her tail to its full extent. She purred lazily and sat upright, her tail wrapped around her neatly.

"We should at least try to rectify the situation. I

know the last thing you want is to leave here. Just letting them get us sent away... That would not be acceptable." Her pronouncement complete, Freya began the ritual washing of the ears.

Molly had never known Freya to agree with the others. If Freya thought this crazy plan worth trying, maybe it had a shot. Molly straightened up and stuck out her chin, with a fresh determination to see this plan through.

Jinks nudged at the door handle, eager as always to get started.

"Come on Molly," he said, remembering to whisper for the moment. "They have to be asleep by now. Let's go!"

The whole gang tiptoed, in their various fashions, across the yard. There was a smattering of clip clopping, a pattering of claws, a padding of paws, a creeping of shoes and an almost silent waddle bringing up the rear.

The shadows lingered across from one end of the yard to the other, draping themselves over the paddock, the sheds, the stable and twisting around the old oak tree. Everything looked strange in the nighttime colors, grays and blacks and the occasional patches of yellow moonlight picking out odd shapes here and there.

In the daytime, Molly knew every inch of the farmyard, but even she felt like a stranger as they crossed from the kitchen to the tree in the corner of the yard, the one which overlooked the garden at number 14. They tiptoed through the night, nose to tail in a line. Long shadows stretched through the dark yard, making the familiar strange and unrecognizable.

A crashing clatter ripped through the heavy silence. The line of animals, and Molly, froze. The clink, clink, clank, gradually died away. The pause lasted for several seconds, until a very sheepish woof broke it.

"Sorry," said Winston. "I knocked the spade over with my tail." Molly could almost hear Freya rolling her eyes in annoyance.

"That dog," she said, a faintly superior purr in her voice, "that dog never knows where to put his paws. Dogs have no grace."

"Quiet everyone," said Molly, as loudly as she dared. She looked around the yard nervously, up at the windows around them, and back at the road behind them. Nothing moved and no lights had blinked on. "Please be more careful, Winston." Molly heard the pleading tone in her own voice. *We've got too much riding on this.*

They all shuffled forward another few feet until the whole pile of them were safely under the old oak. Molly peered up into the shadowy branches to make sure the set up looked as she had left it this morning. The ropes looked as tightly tied as before and the dangling strings of lights hung down clear of the lowest branches.

Please work, Molly thought, *please be alright.* As her eyesight adjusted to the gloom, she saw the rest of the team join them under the tree. Rosemary and Lavender bumbled over to her and nudged Molly's knees with their snouts.

"We're all warmed up my dear and ready for action," said Rosemary.

"Ready for our curtain call," said Lavender.

Molly felt a warm snuffling in her ear. Hampton had appeared behind her. He leaned over Molly's shoulder. She stroked his soft nose and he blew gently in her ear again, the smell of warm hay and carrots on his breath. "Standing by," he said. "I'll round up the sheep." He silently melted away into the shadows.

The windows next door were as dark as their own. A light breeze riffled the leaves above them and Molly shivered. It seemed like a lifetime until they heard a gentle squeak from the sunroom door as it slowly eased open.

"All set," whispered Alastair through the darkness. "Good luck!"

Molly saw his shadow disappear back into the sunroom and out of sight again. She counted slowly to ten to give him enough time to dart back to his room.

Time to start before they all lost their nerve and ran back to hide under her duvet. Molly squared her shoulders and patted the featheriness next to her. "Are you ready, Duck?"

"All ready and willing Molly. Duck to duty, as it were." She saluted smartly with one wing and her tail feathers stood to attention. "Air Corps Surveillance ready for action ma'am." Molly's eyes sparkled as the excitement spread.

"Go for it Air Wing Commander," she said and saluted her back. Duck spread her wings and clumsily ran the length of the yard, mud splattering to either side of her. At the last minute, her wings caught the air current and instead of crashing into the fence, she took off and soared into the air.

"Bravo Air Wing Commander!" said Jinks. They all cheered very quietly until Molly shushed them.

"You next Jinks," she said.

Winston pushed the loose fence panel with his nose until the hole gaped large enough for the goat to trot through. As it slipped back into position, Jinks clip clipped up the paved pathway to the shadow of the sunroom. With a stick held firmly between his strong teeth, he pushed the latch of the glass doors up and they swung open with a gentle creak. He nudged them into the perfect position, to exactly where Freya had put a big cross in the dirt, and with a chuckle, sneaked back to the fence.

From behind the fence, on the farmyard side, Molly and the others heard him muttering and bleating in frustration. A great rustling of leaves, then a muted crash of branches followed by the sound of something heavy being winched down from the tree above, clanking gently as it hit the top of the fence. Jinks tied off the rope and whispered through the fence to the others - "All set here."

"I've got the switch," said Winston.

Hampton tiptoed over to the chickens and the three sheep. He nudged them towards Molly and they skittered around her knees, chattering away in a murmur. Molly bent down and stroked one of the wiry wooled heads. "Keep the noise down everyone. We don't want them waking up before we're ready, do we? Come and line up here, by the fence. No, not under the tree, Mildred. Stand next to Boris; he's in the perfect spot. Bella, are you warm enough there? Not there, Mildred. That's it. Right there. Now don't move, we're waiting for Duck's signal..."

At that very moment, a dark figure swooped low over their heads and then back into the neighbors' garden. Up to the roof she soared, a silent shadow against the darkness of the sky. She landed heavily on the roof and waddled over to the chimney pot at the end of the roof.

"That's it!" Molly whispered. A strange howling came from the roof, echoing down into the chimney. Duck wailed and yowled as if her tail feathers were caught in the door. "Oh! Save me, save me!" she called into the void. "I see the light! Save me!"

A light flicked on at the front of the house. Mr. Henderson had heard the noise. His shadow crossed the window and the hallway light flicked on. The gang of farmyard animals tracked his progress as the lights went on downstairs and into the living room, where the sound echoed from the fireplace. The sound stopped abruptly. Mr. Henderson's voice boomed across the night.

"Who's there? What are you doing on my roof?" he yelled. "Come down from there so I can get a good look at you." Molly could see him through the living room window, as he crossed the room and stuck his head up the chimney to get a better look. "Get down here, whoever you are!"

At that moment, Duck flew straight up from the edge of the roof and settled on the chimney pot. She unclipped a bag from her leg and rolled the strange object to the edge. It was a donkey bomb – a Jinks invention which was made from donkey manure, rolled into the shape of a basketball and baked for several days in the sun. Hard and brittle on the outside, and full of donkey stink on the inside. Perfect for this sort of situation.

Duck edged the donkey bomb over the rim of the chimney pot. It fell straight down and exploded as it hit the floor. A cloud of black soot billowed out of the fireplace, covering Mr. Henderson from head to toe. His marvelous beard was particularly drenched in the smoky powder, the fiery red doused by the gray ash. He roared in anger and then coughed violently as he breathed it all in. Choking for breath, he banged on the chimney breast angrily, which set more soot bursting forth from the opening.

The chickens found this hilarious and could barely breathe from laughing. Cluck, cluck, cluck, rearing up and cackling at the sight of him.

"Shhhhhhh," said Molly, desperate that they shouldn't be heard this time.

But nothing would be heard over the sounds Mr. Henderson made as he clomped blindly around the room, bellowing like an annoyed bull. Mrs. Henderson finally emerged from the bedroom and timidly crept into the soot blackened living room to find her husband causing chaos. She flapped around him trying to calm him down and having the opposite effect. He yelled and she squawked and the chickens clucked with laughter.

Air Commander Duck moved on to Stage Two of the plan. She appeared to be enjoying her new role, thought Molly. Landing precariously in the tree above Molly, she grabbed the harness attached to the ropes of lights and shrugged it on. The lights jangled below her, but Duck stepped carefully so as not to tangle them. Freya posted herself by the switch at the other end of the strings. One paw poised, she watched intently as Duck flew towards the bedroom windows.

Freya pressed the switch, rapidly blinking the fairy lights on, off, on, off. Tiny balls of light flashed brightly, dancing in erratic patterns in the air. From inside the house, it must have looked very odd. From the screeches coming from the bedrooms, Molly knew that Petunia had woken up.

"Muuuuuuuum!" screamed Petunia.

"Daaaaaaaaaaaaaaad!" yelled Alastair, as loudly as possible to add to the chaos. Molly could see him at the bedroom window, listening hard to what the others were doing and ruffling his hair to look as if he had just woken up.

Mrs. Henderson abandoned her husband in his crisis and hared up the stairs to her precious little darlings. Mr. Henderson lumbered up the stairs behind her, crashing into every door, wall and piece of furniture on the way. As they reached the top, Molly signaled to the chickens. Bella and the others began to peck at the buttons on the tiny sound board with enthusiasm.

Noises seeped out from random places all over the garden. Howls and screeches pierced the night, followed by long shuddering rolls of thunder. Even Molly felt a bit unnerved by it all, and she was responsible for the chaos. As the noises swelled, Molly pointed to the sheep. The trio of woolly heads huddled together and began to sing. A three-part harmony of ghastly groans filled the air and drifted across the garden.

"What is all this nonsense?" shouted Mr. Henderson. "Be quiet you lot! Shut up!" His family fell silent, but all the screeching, howling, groaning and thunder went right on happening. He growled angrily and tore back down the stairs to the sunroom.

"Now!" said Molly, as loudly as she could. Duck swooped overhead, lights off, to land behind them. Winston bent forward and flicked the switch he gripped between his paws and the ghost came to life. It wasn't really a ghost of course, only Jinks in a white flowing dress. But to three of the Hendersons, rushing downstairs in a panic, a real-life ghost had emerged from their vegetable patch. Alastair stood at the back of the group, his hand clapped over his mouth to hold in his laughter.

The ghostly figure glided gently along, moaning and groaning theatrically. Petunia screamed. Mrs. Henderson fainted elegantly into a wicker chair. Mr. Henderson's face burned redder than his beard. He roared again at the ghostly image and rushed at the door, shaking his fist at the pale image."

"It's Aunt Mildred!" he yelled. "Mildred - you come back here. I want to know what you did with the family emeralds. Where did you hide your will? Who was supposed to get the silver cutlery? I know it wasn't Desmond. You come here, right now, Mildred, and answer my questions. Being dead isn't going to help you - I want answers!" He hurled himself through the sunroom door and into the pitch blackness outside, stumbling in bare feet on the sharp gravel.

Quick as a wink, Winston switched off the light and hauled it up out of sight. "Let me in, let me in." Jinks banged heavily on the fence with his horns, trying to find the loose panel. "He's right behind me." Molly pushed the fence open and Jinks dashed through, breathing very heavily for a ghost.

"Where are those darn ghosts? I saw you - I saw you Aunt Mildred. You come back here now - I want a word with you." They could hear him crashing and banging around in the garden. "You get back here now!"

Molly, Duck, Winston, Bella and Jinks tiptoed back to their own kitchen silently. Molly sank into a wooden chair and shook with laughter that they had got away with such a daring plan. Eventually, Molly persuaded the animals to sneak off to their various beds, kennels, pens and coops for a couple of hours of sleep, confident that their glorious plan had scared the Henderson family into moving away. They couldn't have been more wrong.

CHAPTER TWENTY

A Visit from the Hendersons

It began with a violent hammering on the door knocker at half past six in the morning. On any normal morning at the farmyard, this wouldn't have met with any surprise. But this was the morning after the Big Spooky Plan, which had kept some of them up half the night.

Mrs. Flabbergast herself was still recovering from a full day of filming an advertisement for toothpaste which had involved two of the chickens, Robbie the Rooster, Donald the donkey, and Daisy - the cow with the biggest smile. None of them, including the animals, had particularly relished waking up for the five o'clock alarms that morning. Even Robbie had half opened one eye and shut it determinedly for another half hour of sleep.

When the door-knocker got no answer, he tried

banging on the door. Great heavy fist falls on the old wood added to the hundreds of dents already decorating the peeling red paint. Mr. Henderson flung open the letterbox and bellowed through the slot. "I know you're in there," he shouted. "We can see the lights on. You come out here right now and apologize. We know it was you and your animals last night. But you won't get away with it."

Molly stared down from her bedroom window at the scene below.

"Oh Freya," she said, "I don't think our plan worked after all. He's not scared, he's angry. I think we may have made things even worse." The cat strolled along the windowsill, rubbing her back against Molly's shoulder. She peered down at the top of four heads and hissed, her mouth flaring and nose turning up.

"They're bad people Molly. They're going to make us move whatever we do."

"Maybe they're not bad people exactly. Alastair's OK. He's on our side. Perhaps they don't like us because we're so very different from them." Molly struggled to find something positive to say about the Hendersons.

"You mean, we're nice?" Freya sneered at the head tops. "I could be less nice," she said. "I could drop dead mice in their mouths when they're asleep. Or put a snake in their beds. Or stick a bird in their bathroom. If they want us to be just like them."

Molly shook her head slowly. "I don't think we need to be nasty, Freya. That wouldn't change their minds about us and it won't fix the problem would it? The thing is, I've run out of ideas and today is already Thursday. Tomorrow afternoon, Mr. Bennet will be back and the Henderson family are going to have more complaints, not less. He's going to find a hundred reasons to say we've failed the inspection, and then he's going to evict us."

Molly sniffed loudly, and turned away from Freya. The bedsprings creaked as the girl sank onto the edge of the bed.

"I hope we haven't made them so angry that they ask to have Grandma's license for the farm taken away. It's going to be terrible enough if we have to leave here, and my dad not being able to find us..." she paused, trying so hard not to break down. Reaching out towards the frame on her nightstand, Molly picked it up and stroked the photograph. Carefully, she reset the frame next to the lamp.

"But the thought of losing everyone to zoos and shelters...." A tear gave up and slid slowly down her check.

Freya's eyes closed to slits. Anyone who could upset her Molly like this deserved a whole pillow full of dead mice, as far as she was concerned. She stared down at the head tops again, wondering if they were trying to break the front door down.

To judge by the scene below, this was a distinct possibility. Mrs. Henderson stood with her arms crossed, one toe tapping the floor as if leading a marching band. Petunia stood behind her, nose in the air and smirking as if Christmas had come early, with extra candy canes. Several net curtains twitched at the windows along the street, as various neighbors tried to see who the obnoxious family were bullying now. Petunia caught a glimpse of Mrs. Joseph peeking at them, and waved at her shamelessly, loving the attention.

"Yoo-hoo! Mrs. Joseph! How wonderful to see you - you really should come out and enjoy the sunrise. Oh, and there's dear little Ravi!" She flapped frantically at the wide-eyed boy as he peered out from the upstairs window at number 10.

"Sis, stop it, it's bad enough with Dad throwing a fit." Alastair appeared to be trying to merge into the hedge. His cheeks flamed pink under the generous smattering of freckles and clashing with the carroty color of his hair. Freya thought he looked like a traffic light against the green of the hedge wrapping its branches around him.

Mr. Henderson was on the verge of exploding. His hair stood on end where he had shoved his hands through it so many times. Sweat dripped down the sides of his face. His beard stood out from his face as if electrified. He jumped up and down and alternated between yelling through the letterbox and ringing the doorbell as loudly as he could. The red alarm lights flashed silently above Molly's door, set off anew every time Mr. Henderson hit the doorbell.

"Come out here now where I can yell at you!" he shouted.

To everyone's surprise, including Mr. Henderson's, the battered red door opened. A chicken or two fell out onto the doorstep, followed by a curious Duck who quacked around the feet of the visitors and peered up at their surprise.

"Hello?" said a disembodied voice from below Molly's bedroom. "I'm so sorry; I don't think I heard you knock. Can I help you at all?"

"Uh oh," said Molly, her ears alert to the sound of her grandmother's voice. The tears stopped as quickly as they had started, and she wiped her dripping nose with the back of her sleeve. *I guess it's time for business*, she thought.

"She doesn't know what we did Freya. She won't know what they're talking about. Grandma will probably tell them they're crazy. That will only make it worse."

The cat and the girl scooted off the bed and ran for the stairs. Molly hurled herself down them two at a time, trying not to get all tangled up in a helpful cat, to reach her grandmother before she said the wrong thing. They skidded on the slick tiles at the kitchen entrance, caught the door frame and slid down the hallway, coming to a halt inches behind Mrs. Flabbergast. Molly could nearly see steam coming from Mr. Henderson's ears as her grandma tried to reason with him. His hands clenched and unclenched and he snarled back at them.

"No, I do not want a cup of tea," he said. "Or a rhubarb and ... cucumber custard." His nose wrinkled at the thought of it.

"Well, I think I could do with one," said Mrs. Flabbergast. "Do go and put the kettle on Molly, there's a good girl."

Molly opened her mouth to explain to her grandmother. *How on earth can I do that?* But the old lady turned and winked at her.

"Now, please Molly. I'm sure this won't take long." She nodded towards the kitchen.

Molly had no choice but to back up through the hallway, leaving Freya to weave in and out of her grandmother's legs and purr aggressively at the neighbors. The cat slunk around the shouting Mr. Henderson and made her way over to Alastair.

"Did you tell them?" she muttered at him, under cover of the shouting.

"No! Not a word." He went even brighter red and bent down to her, as if trying to scratch between her ears. "I'm sorry Freya, he's furious. I don't know what..."

"Leave that animal alone!" said Mrs. Henderson. "Dirty creatures, all of them."

Molly could hear every word of the conversation through the open kitchen door.

"You and that girl have done it now," shouted Mr. Henderson. "I've had enough of your tricks. You invaded our home yesterday and made ghosts happen."

Mrs. Flabbergast put on her sweetest voice. "Oh no, my dear Mr. Henderson. You must be mistaken. We were out all day yesterday filming a curious television advertisement for toothpaste. I brought Molly with me of course, she's the only one Daisy will listen to. No point using a cow who won't smile to show off her teeth to sell toothpaste now is there?" Molly's lips pinched together as she listened to her grandma lying through her teeth for her. She took the tin kettle over to the big white sink, clanking noisily so everyone could hear her doing as she was told. Under cover of the sound of water splashing loudly into metal, Molly crept back towards the doorway.

"You're not making a lot of sense, Mr. Henderson. You say that there were ghosts in your house last night and you somehow think that Molly had something to do with it? Molly is good with cows, but I don't know how much control she has over ghosts."

"Ghosts!" said Mrs. Henderson, almost stuttering with excitement. "Ghosts. We h'are not the type to have ghosts!"

Mr. Henderson shook his head furiously. "I know you're making fun of me Mrs. Flabbergast, but I know that girl is responsible. We never had ghosts before. We're a respectable family. Not the type to have ghosts. So they must have come from your property."

"Dear me, you make them sound like mice. I'm sure we're not the type to have ghosts either, and if we did, I don't think we would share them with you. Goodbye now." With that, Mrs. Flabbergast shut the door firmly in the faces of the neighbors. Molly heard a roar from the other side and then silence. She sneaked back to the overflowing kettle.

"Molly." Her Grandma spoke quietly from the doorway. "Did you have anything to do with ghosts next door?" She peered over the top of her spectacles at Molly and raised her eyebrows.

I can't lie to her, thought Molly. *Grandma always knows when she isn't being told everything. It's practically a superpower.*

"Ghosts?" she said, her eyes wide and eyelashes fluttering.

"Hmmmm," said Mrs. Flabbergast, crossing the room to settle herself in her rocking chair by the stove. She opened the stove door, shoved in a couple of logs and rattled around the poker to get the flames moving again. "Get that kettle on and you can tell me all about it over a nice cup of tea."

Molly did exactly that. She explained about the lights and the noises down the chimney and the special ghost effect starring Jinks. Mrs. Flabbergast nodded and rocked in her rickety old rocking chair. She sipped her tea and chuckled as Molly went further back and told her all about the first attack they had launched on the Hendersons and their green tongues and itchy spots.

"Oh Molly, that's wonderful," Mrs. Flabbergast said, wiping the tears of laughter from her cheeks. "Apart from breaking into the neighbors' house."

"Only the first time. The second time, Alastair left the door open for us."

"Alastair did? The Henderson boy?"

"Yes. He's actually OK. He doesn't want us to leave either, and he wants to stop his parents getting us kicked out."

"Oh." The chair squeaked back and forth a few times. "But why on earth didn't you tell me about all this before you did it?"

"We didn't want to get you into trouble. Jinks

said that if you didn't know about it, even if it all went wrong, they couldn't take your farm license away. Even if we still had to move, you would still be able to keep the Flabbergast Farm itself going somehow, and keep doing all the TV and film work."

"That silly goat," said her grandmother. "I don't think Mr. Bennet would really take my farm license away, do you? He just wants us to be somewhere else so he doesn't have to deal with us and all our noises and smells and muddy puddles." She stopped rocking and the chair gradually slowed to stillness. Mrs. Flabbergast's shoulders drooped and for a moment, Molly could see all of her seventy-four years on her. "I do wish we didn't have to move though," she said quietly. "So many memories of your grandfather are here in this house for me. Then your dad as a boy here. And you as a littl'un."

The room sat silent for a minute. Molly had no idea what to say. But the stillness wrapped around her, warm and comforting. The grandfather clock tick tocked in the hallway. Logs crackled in the stove. Eventually the creak as the rocking chair began to move again. Those were the sounds of home. *What would another house sound like?* Molly wondered. *Probably not the same.*

"You know," said Mrs. Flabbergast into the stillness, "I think you had the right idea. But you needed to think bigger. Much, much bigger…."

CHAPTER TWENTY-ONE

Alerting the TV Crews

The next morning, tempted by the smell of a sizzling frying pan, Molly crept downstairs to see her grandmother handling the telephone and a spatula with busy hands. She flipped eggs, poured tea and kept moving, but as she moved, she shoveled words into the ears of whoever listened at the other end of the line. The exhaustion of the previous day had gone, and her grandmother was filled with fire.

Molly wouldn't have recognized her grandmother by the voice alone. Her voice rumbled deeper than usual and filled with the richness of the Welsh mountains.

"Oh yes, boyo, we've seen some funny stuff

around here. You should come and take a good look at it, you should. Yes, it was a goat!" A brief pause as some unseen person on the other end of the line finally got a word in, then Mrs. Flabbergast continued. "Yes, a goat. With horns and a tail. Exactly. I don't know how long he's been here - you'd have thought he'd be hard to hide wouldn't you? No, I don't think he's dangerous, but you never know really, with goats, do you now? If you come along now, you might be able to catch him at it. Talking away, blabbering on. Thank you, lovely, we'll be expecting you."

Molly crept another couple of steps down and heard the phone being dialed again. This time the voice pitched higher, melodic, wrapping words around a strong Cornish accent. "Is that Median TV? Yes, I need to speak to the news desk.... Would you like to hear about the talking goat I've found in the middle of Suburbia?" Molly listened, puzzled by her grandmother's strange voices, to the old lady appealing to several different television studios and news channels. Each one got the same odd story from her of a talking goat accosting them in Chestnut Grove this morning and demanding that someone come and interview her immediately.

***

"He wanted my hat of all things!" she said sharply and slammed down the phone with great satisfaction. "You can come out now Molly," she said in her normal voice. "I've called about twenty television crews, and four or five should be on their way immediately. You would think they'd all be rushing here, wouldn't you? After all, nothing tops a talking goat. Except maybe a laughing llama and I have one of those as backup."

"But apparently, some of them thought I invented it! Here you go Bella, your turn. I'll dial the number and you can add some extra voices, I think they've heard all of mine. The trick is, to talk your way past the receptionist, who doesn't believe anything, and get to the reporters, who believe everything." Bella hopped up onto the kitchen table and shuffled her way along to the phone receiver. "There you go girl!"

"Do you think I should start with my BBC announcer voice?" asked the chicken. "Is that my best one do you think?" she worried. "Or I could try my Birmingham accent... What do you think Molly?"

"I'm sorry," said Molly, "I don't really understand." She dragged the wooden chair away from the worn kitchen table and plonked herself down in it. She propped her head in her hands and stared at her grandmother. "You've always said we must never let anyone know that the animals can talk. But this morning you are practically advertising it on the morning news?"

"Change of tactics dear. No one will ever really believe it, but they do love a good story and will be dying to know how it's done. If we can get them all here and thinking that we have talking animals, there's no way the general public will let Mr.

Bennet take away our license. It might make us even more famous. Now, we must get everything ready before you go to school." She shoved a fried egg and cucumber sandwich into Molly's hand and pushed her towards the back door.

"School?" said Molly. "You expect me to go to school on a day like today? I have to be here. We have to save the farm and the license and make sure Mr. Bennet doesn't shut us down."

"I appreciate your help, Molly dear, but I really think the best thing you can do is go to school. If you skip class and then your teacher sees you on the News channel, I don't think that will really help our cause, now will it?"

"But you need me Grandma. I have to help."

"Oh, I think we'll manage just fine, thank you Molly. It's straightforward. I'm sure things might change a bit afterwards, but we've really been very lucky keeping our little secret for as long as we have. It's decided, my girl, and you're going to have to let me sort it all out. Now, you run along and get Hampton brushed down first, then Donald needs his hat fixed, and Jinks' teeth should be cleaned. I think if you could give the pigs a nice spray down that would help. Come on Molly, we don't have much time before your bus." She shooed her out into the farmyard and scurried off back inside to dial phone numbers for Bella.

***

Molly stomped across the farmyard, her cheeks flushed red and her hair escaping from her braids as she tugged at them.

The chug-chug-chug of the Hendersons" SUV roaring into life broke the unnatural quiet of the farmyard. Molly looked up to see Alastair standing by the car. His hand rested lightly on the passenger door handle, and his shoulders drooped.

His school uniform is big enough for him to grow into, thought Molly. *Probably, next year. That boy always looks miserable, sad about something. Even about going to that fancy school.* Then Alastair's head shot up and he looked directly at her, as if he'd heard Molly's thoughts. He grinned, his whole face lighting up for a second.

"Get in the car, boy!" his father barked from the driver's seat. "We'll be late."

Typical, thought Molly. *Going off to school when there's real work to be done.*

But Alastair risked a brief wave at her, then yanked open the door and spoke loudly enough for Molly to hear him. "Dad, I feel awful. I think I'm going to be sick."

"Not in my car, you're not. Get back in the house right now. I'll call your school."

Molly grinned as she watched them both traipse back into the house. But then she remembered that she'd been dismissed by her grandma and still had to go to school herself. She glared at Robbie as she passed him. The rooster was perched on the fencepost at the end of the pig pen. He crowed happily at Molly.

"What do you think Molly? Should I wear my new green waistcoat for my television appearance today? Or maybe the blue? My ladies do love me in the blue one. It is a chance to find a whole new group of fans after all. Do you think people who watch the news will already have seen me?" He strutted up and down the railing and pecked at a couple of his wing feathers, ruffling them and puffing himself up. "A whole new audience Molly, all waiting to see me."

"I heard they were supposed to be coming to hear Jinks speak," said Molly. *Not that I'll go*, she thought. *I'm staying here. They think they can do all this without me. Let them then. They can go and live in the country and I'll move into the old oak tree in a tree house.*

Robbie realized she wasn't paying attention to him. He crowed loudly in her ear and cocked his head on one side to look eye to beady eye with Molly.

"Jinks? Well, yes, mainly. I suppose. But the ladies will love me when they see me. I'm going to perch here and stick out my tail feathers like this and fan out my coxcomb like that. See, they're going to be so impressed. And then I thought I'd start singing. Maybe something by Elchick, or The Beetles perhaps. What do you think?" He strutted once more, up and down the fence rail with his beak high in the air.

"I think that if everybody starts showing off, you're going to mess everything up. That's what I think. Not that I'm allowed to have an opinion of course. But I don't think any of you know what she's doing. I mean, calling the news crews here and letting Jinks talk. Jinks! He could say anything. You're going to all end up in zoos and circuses and places like that and made to talk all day. Not that I know anything of course." Molly's hands were clenched. A bead of sweat sprinted down her back and she shivered.

"It's always Jinks that gets to do this sort of thing," grumbled the rooster, his red coxcomb sinking. "When does it get to be the rooster's turn?" Molly thrust her hands into her pockets and backed away from him. "Oooh - I know! A bit of Empress would be perfect for this! What about "We Are the Chickens" or "Another One Bites the Hay?" What do you think?"

"Robbie, I don't have time to argue with you. Grandma's given me a list as long as your.... wing to get done before I'm supposed to go to school. I have to see to Hampton for starters and get him all cleaned up." She turned away from the rooster and headed for the stables. *A rooster singing Queen, for goodness' sake. That's not odd at all.*

As she rounded the corner to the stable door, Donald stuck his head over the top of it and chewed thoughtfully at her.

"Is this a good idea Molly? What if they realize we really can talk. That it's not a trick? What will happen then? I'm quite worried about this, you know."

"I know, I don't get it either. But that's her entire plan apparently. I won't be here to help you when it goes wrong either. Do you have your sunflower hat ready, or do I need to fix that too?" Donald gave her a curious look then trotted over to his board of hats and stuck his head into the special straw one, preening and turning to show off the new silk sunflower attached to the brim of it. "Well, you're fine then," said Molly. "Now shove up so I can get in and brush down Hampton."

The donkey carefully backed up into the corner of the stable so Molly could squeeze past. She peered into Hampton's stall but it was empty of horses. "Where is he?" she asked.

"He went for a walk to clear his head. I think all this stress is getting to him."

"He's not the only one. But he can't go wandering off like this."

"Sorry Molly," said Donald quietly. But Molly had stormed off too quickly to hear him.

CHAPTER TWENTY-TWO

A Terrible Script

Molly checked the pig pen, the paddock, the old oak tree. No Hampton lurking behind, or even in, the chicken coop. "How is it even possible to lose an enormous horse in such a small farmyard?" she muttered. The vegetable garden and the back of the shed were also horse-free. Finally, she stuck her head round the corner of the Land rover and got a face full of Hampton's rear end. Molly sputtered at him through a mouthful of horsetail. "What are you doing Hampton? I've been looking everywhere for you."

The horse looked sideways at her. "Practicing my lines," he said, reluctantly.

"Your lines?"

"Mrs. Flabbergast has written an entire script for us to learn. She's a wonderful lady, your grandmother, but I'm not sure that scriptwriting is one of her talents. I'm supposed to give a monologue about racing down the beach at sunset. Do I look like I race?" He kicked up his enormous front hooves. "I'm built for pulling carts of hay, not running around on sand. Speaking of which, what is sand like? I've never been on a beach. Have you been to the beach Molly?"

Molly went pale. The last time she had gone to the beach, she had ridden on her Daddy's shoulders. Her ice cream had melted and dripped on his hair. He had laughed and wiped it off. Molly remembered his smile as she looked down at him, her fingers curled tight in his long brown hair, the same color and thickness as hers.

"Molly?" Hampton snapped at her. "What are you planning to do about this? I mean, one has a reputation to uphold. I cannot be seen performing a script this awful. How would this look on my professional resume? I'm a carthorse. Racehorse on beach - that sounds so amateur. You really must speak to your grandmother."

"I tried to speak to her already, Hampton. She said I had to go to school."

"Harrumph. That's ridiculous. You can't go waltzing off to school, young lady. We have important matters to attend to here. Don't you go deserting us on a day like today. I would be most disappointed in you if you did that."

"I don't think I have a choice, Hampton. What I do have, however, is a long to do list. You're at the top of it. Grandmother wants you groomed and looking smart before the TV crews arrive."

"I don't have time for that, Molly. I told you, I have lines to learn. Ridiculous lines. It's a part for a racehorse, not a carthorse. I don't know who she thinks..." Hampton turned away from her, muttering loudly about the unfairness of it all. Molly realized that nothing she could say would persuade him back to the stables for a clean-up and brush.

"Well, fine," she said. "Be like that then. No one else listens to me, so why should you?"

***

She stomped off towards the pigpen.

"I'm not getting splattered in mud," said Rosemary.

"Nor I," chimed in Lavender. "We're as clean as a whistle right now, and I do not want nasty, sticky, dirty mud all over my beautiful pink silk scarf."

Rosemary snuffled in agreement. "Oh, that is a nice scarf, Lavender. Wherever did you get that?"

"Why, thank you, Rosemary. Mrs. Flabbergast gave it to me. She said I should look ethereal in it, whatever that means."

"I think it means ghostly," said Rosemary, her snout wrinkling in confusion. "Why on earth would she want you to look like a ghost?"

"Do you know, I have no idea. It doesn't say anything about that in the scri..." Rosemary cannoned into her before she could finish the sentence. "What did you do that for dear girl? I only mentioned..." She paused to listen to

Rosemary, who had stuck her snout into Lavender's silky left ear and started whispering forcefully. "Oh. Oh, yes that's right. No, I shouldn't say. Sorry dear." They both turned and looked sharply at Molly, as if she were the one who had nearly let the cat out of the bag. "It's alright," she said. "I know about the script. Hampton told me all about it. He's not happy about it."

The pigs exchanged glances. Rosemary gave in first and tried to explain nicely to Molly. "It's not that it's a bad script as such...." she began.

"Oh, it is," interrupted Lavender. "It's a very bad script. It's so awful I wouldn't even line our - you know - "unhygienic corner" with it." The ladies were running an ongoing campaign for an outdoor lavatory for their personal use, but so far it had resulted in a corner of the pen being lined with old newspaper and hidden behind a decorative screen. The unhygienic corner was where documents issued by Mr. Bennet often ended up.

"Why? What does she have you two doing?" asked Molly, curious now as to how bad this script could be.

"Traditional Irish folk songs," said Lavender, her voice flat and unemotional. "All in the key of D major, one octave, no vibrato. I mean, dear, is there any point even warming up?"

"I do feel we're missing an opportunity. Really, when you have pigs with our vocal range, why would you not want to stage "La Traviata" for the cameras?"

Molly frowned. It felt like her grandmother

planned to reveal their biggest secret to the world in a way that showed them at their worst. It made no sense, no sense at all.

"I don't know," she said to the affronted pigs. "I don't understand it at all. But I do know that she asked me to give you two a bath. We should get on with that."

"I don't think we'll need a bath thank you deary. We'll just finish tidying ourselves up. I'm sure you have more urgent things to attend to," said Rosemary. "Don't you have to get to school, dear?"

With that, Molly was dismissed. The pigs watched her all the way out.

CHAPTER TWENTY-THREE

Molly and Duck

Molly wandered over to sit in the chair by her fairy grotto. The farmyard was the only place she felt part of it all, not left out on her own. She felt her stomach sinking as she watched the animals bustle past, each with a purpose. Molly sniffed loudly. She could feel the tears prickling at her eyes, and shuffled further back on the chair. Right onto a very quiet Duck.

"Watch out!" she quacked at Molly and shuffled off the chair. "Some of us are trying to have a nap in all this chaos." Molly sniffed again, but she didn't quite trust herself to speak yet. Instead, she nodded and turned away from Duck.

"There's no need to be rude about it," snapped the sleepy Duck. Then she saw the tear slip slowly down Molly's cheek. "Oh," she said, in a softer voice. "What's wrong?"

Molly shook her head. All the things that had gone wrong in the last week piled up and teetered over her in a great wobbling heap of fear and misery. Everything she loved and cherished, the one place she felt safe, was being threatened. Worse, her best friends wouldn't let her help save the day. Molly had run out of words for it all. A second tear joined the first.

"I'm so sorry Molly. I didn't mean to shout." The awkward pause lengthened.

"It's OK," Molly said, sniffing back the other tears. "I didn't see you there. Sorry for sitting on you."

"That's OK. Are you getting stressed about the television people coming? I thought I'd sit over here until Mrs. Flabbergast calls me. I get in the way apparently. Have you learned your lines yet?"

"I don't have any lines. I won't even be here. I'm expected to go to school and pretend everything is fine. The single thing they've told me is that they're going to let the TV reporters know that all the animals can talk. Oh, and that the script, the one that is supposed to save our farm, is terrible."

Duck nodded sadly. "It is pretty bad. I do get to do a short martial arts demonstration, but really it's more 'Karate Kid' than true ninja duck moves. The sort of thing I learned as a duckling, nothing challenging at all."

"It's almost as if we're showing the world that you can all talk and sing and, well, ninja. But then we're showing them that you do it really badly."

"Yeah, so no-one's going to hire us after this. We

might get to keep the farm for a while, but if we don't get any work after this, we'll have to move eventually anyway. I'm going to miss doing karate movies," said Duck. "Especially the bits where I do my own voice-overs."

"I can't see how this is going to stop Mr. Bennet taking our license. In fact, he's more likely to. I bet he doesn't have a box he can tick labeled "Talking Animals". I mean, is that it? Is that her whole plan? She's hoping that the general public will be up in arms at the thought of closing us down, and march down here to force Mr. Bennet to give us our license. Is there more to it? She's being so secretive."

"Oh." Duck fanned out her feathers and resettled herself. She didn't know quite what to say to Molly. Everyone had been given their instructions except, apparently, for Molly. "I don't know, to be honest, my dear. I think that's about as far as she got. Mrs. Flabbergast has given out some directions to some of us, but not a lot of details to anyone. She only told me about my job. I have to fly out from the tree when Lavender cries out something about umbrellas, and then the Doctor appears in the frame, and then.... There's a bit where I karate chop Jinks. I think there was a roundhouse kick at one point. It gets a bit confusing to be honest. Why won't she let you stay home and help?"

"She gave me a long list of things to do and told me to go and get on with them before school." Molly sighed.

Duck stared long and hard at her. She had

known Molly since her duckling days and had never known Molly to give up or give in about anything. "I don't think that's very fair. I wonder if Freya has any suggestions...?"

"Actually, I do." The velvety voice made them both jump. Freya slunk out of the shadows and curled around the fairy grotto to leap up onto Molly's lap. She butted her head against the girl's pale cheeks and patted her shoulder gently with one paw. "How ridiculous that is, trying to send you to school today. We need you, Molly. You need to save the farm today, and then you'll still be here to go on Monday. Sometimes grown-ups can be so short sighted about those sorts of things."

Molly smiled weakly at the cat. "Did you have an idea then Freya?"

"Well if you can dial the number for me, I can at least talk to the school for you, and then I thought we could put our heads together about our other problem. I know you'll come up with something when we really need it."

"I'm working on it. But this plan of Grandma's isn't giving me much time." Molly paused. One thought had occurred to her. "Freya?"

The cat pricked up an ear.

"Do you think there's any chance Dad could see us? If we were on the telly?"

"It's possible. I don't know if there are any national news people coming. But there's always a chance." Freya slid gracefully down from Molly's lap to the floor and slunk off in the direction of the farmhouse to use the telephone.

Molly blinked back the tears which were creeping back behind her eyes. They had no time for that now. She couldn't give up - the animals needed her to think of something. With a plan as awful as her grandmother's, Molly had to come up with something amazing, and quickly. Her mind went blank.

She jumped as a strange noise came from the fence in front of her. It sounded like a giant rat scrabbling its way up the wood, but then Alastair's face appeared, red and sweaty, above the top of the fence.

"Are you OK?" he asked, frowning at Molly. "I'm really sorry about my dad yelling yesterday. I tried to stop him..."

"I don't have time for all that," snapped Molly. "Grandma's called in all the local TV crews to see our talking animals. It's a last-ditch attempt to save the farm, but it means they're going to all be taken away from us."

Alastair thought for a minute. "All your animals? You mean, it isn't just the cat who can talk?"

Molly nodded slowly. It was going to be all over the news today anyway.

"Wow! I had no idea. Wow! OK, OK, OK. What are we going to do then? We can't let that happen."

Molly sighed. "It's no use, I've run out of ideas, and what's it to you anyway? Why do you care if we get kicked out?"

"Seriously? I've just found out that I live next door to the coolest animals ever, and you think I don't care if you move! You're not too awful either I suppose." He blushed even redder at this and looked away.

Molly stared at him. "Anything helpful to suggest then?" She sniffed away the last of the tears. *At least I'm not completely on my own,* she thought. *Even if he is a boy.*

"I wish," said Alastair. "But I don't think anything will make him back down now. He's really mad at you. And he always gets what he wants. You've seen our house. New sunroom, extra satellite dishes, a new shed, an extra bedroom. My dad just decides we have to have all that to show everyone else how much better we are. It's stupid. He just decides and then they get built."

"Don't be daft," said Molly. "That stuff always takes ages. The forms, the applications, the inspections. Trust me; it took eleven months to get the planning permission for Hampton's stable. You can't just stick a new room on."

"Well, my dad does. He doesn't bother with all that sort of stuff," said Alastair gloomily. "He says that sort of thing only applies to other people. He thinks he's being clever."

"Oh, does he?" Molly looked up at the Henderson house towering over their own little farm.

That house is getting bigger and bigger, she thought. *Bigger and bigger…* Molly's eyes gleamed as a plan formed.

CHAPTER TWENTY-FOUR

Llama in the Limelight

"Lights, camera, action!" declared Mrs. Flabbergast.

Only the eyes behind the TV cameras rolled at her, and a young assistant jumped forward with her clipboard, waving her hands. She was probably the fourth such assistant Molly had seen, and they all looked the same. Battered cargo trousers, the pockets stuffed with pens and walkie talkies and sheets of papers; over-sized tee-shirts bearing a once funny joke, and shoulder length hair scraped back unsuccessfully into a ponytail.

The only way to tell them apart is by reading their tee-shirts, thought Molly.

Molly had hidden from her grandmother and the

huge crowd who were trampling her beloved farmyard. She'd pretended to go off to school and then concealed herself behind the chicken coop until Freya had given the all clear. Molly knew the chickens would never rat on her. She shifted position quietly to stop her legs falling asleep underneath her and tried to edge round the corner to see better.

"No, no, no, Mrs. Flabbergast. We've been through this. I'm going to call the 3, 2 and show you the 1. I'll do that. You stay there and be ready for when I do this. OK?" - Miss 'Don't ask me till I've had my coffee' waited for the nod of understanding from the older lady and then backed up behind the camera, ready to try again.

Molly surveyed the chaos in her farmyard.

Fourteen television cameras had shown up, complete with their operators, sound people, production assistants, and various other random people attached. Then there were the newspaper reporters and their photographers, and who knows who else. Molly had given up trying to count all of them. The line of aerial covered vans stretched all down the crescent, as far as she could see. More were still arriving.

***

"Good afternoon, everyone. My name is Eugenia Flabbergast and I run the Flabbergast Farm here at Chestnut Crescent. It's time that I introduced everyone to some of our amazing animals who live here with me."

Behind the coop, Molly covered her mouth with her hands and shook her head sadly. *I can't believe that Grandma could go through with this. She's exposing our biggest secret to the whole world. It's going to be the end of everything!*

Mrs. Flabbergast launched into her best impression of a helpless little old lady. One who never got up to tricks and mischief. She waved vaguely at the farmyard around her and continued in a wibbly wobbly voice.

"I would like you to meet Donald, our resident donkey, and Rosemary and Lavender, two examples of Gloucester Old Spots, a traditional breed of pig. Behind me, here, is..." she waved vaguely in the direction of an impatient goat.

Jinks stood a few feet behind her, already bored with the waiting. He shifted from one hoof to another, and then another. Ears twitching, Jinks searched the audience for a promising target.

One of the reporters shoved a microphone under Mrs. Flabbergast's nose. "Yes, but what is so special about these animals, Mrs. Flabbergast? We were promised a shocking story!"

The others chimed in, desperate to know that this hadn't just been a stunt to generate publicity for the Flabbergast Farm. They couldn't go back to their stations, tails between their legs as it were, with a story about there being animals on a farm. Their editors and producers would have all been furious with them. The noise level rose to an angry roar.

Jinks decided to take matters in hand. "Excuse me," he said, his loud braying voice cutting through the general hubbub. Everyone turned to everyone else to see who had spoken.

Jinks! No! What are you doing? thought Molly. *You crazy goat!*

"Over here," said Jinks. Confused, the crowd looked over there. But they saw only a tattered looking goat staring back at them.

"Yes. That's right," said Jinks. "Talking animals. She thought you should know. Thought it might make a good story. We tried to dissuade her, but the ladies wanted to see their faces in the newspaper." Rosemary and Lavender simpered coquettishly at the photographers and batted their long eyelashes.

"And Robbie the Rooster and his fine following" - Robbie bowed smartly as Jinks mentioned him - "are always keen on meeting new fans. So, we thought, why not? What's the worst that could happen?"

The crowd surged forward as they realized that the goat really was talking. Hands shot up and reporters thrust microphones under his nose.

What a wonderful time he's having, thought Molly. *For now, until they drag him away to perform in a circus.*

"Absolutely," agreed Mrs. Flabbergast. "Over here is Winston, our Old English Sheepdog. And behind you is Larry the Llama. He's not very chatty though, at least not until he's had his coffee in the mornings."

Larry leaned across the reporter he had sneaked up on and snatched the recording machine from between her fingers. He watched her thoughtfully as he crunched up the whole machine carefully and slowly, finally spewing the contraption out on the floor and spitting heartily after it.

"Not chatty, but quite grumpy. Still, what can you expect from a llama?" she went on cheerfully.

The reporter stared open mouthed at first Larry and then Mrs. Flabbergast. Then back to Larry. He winked at her cheekily, his long dark eyelashes fluttering up and down, and ambled past her to join the others, stomping the remains of the recording machine into the mud as he went.

"Not grumpy. Hungry." Larry boomed. At least they assumed it was Larry's voice. The crowd of heads whipped round to stare at the llama.

"You have a goat and a llama who can speak?" said the quickest reporter. Camilla Hughes had a reputation for believing anything, and her channel was famous for reporting the unbelievable. For once, this gave her a huge advantage over the others. She elbowed her way to the front of the pack and took charge whilst everyone else stood gawking at the idea.

"Tell me, Mrs. Flabbergast, and the Channel 12 viewers, how did these animals learn to talk? Where did they come from? Did you teach them?" The pound signs flashed in Camilla's eyes as she realized the potential of this story. She would grab the exclusives, photo shoots, interviews, speaking tours, and make a fortune from this. She straightened her powder blue jacket and popped the cuffs, fluffed her hair and prepared for battle.

"Do you have an agent yet? Have you given any interviews?" She pounded away with her questions and no one else could get a word in. Including Mrs. Flabbergast.

Chaos, thought Molly. She nervously pulled on one, then the other of her braids. They were already starting to escape into a frizzy tangle as Molly's fingers fiddled with them. *Grandma really has not thought this through. How could this... spectacle... save the farmyard? The risk of losing the animals is enormous. What good could ever come of telling the world our animals can talk? Whatever happens now, the news of the talking animals will already be out in the world. There's no way it can be hushed up now.*

But then an unexpected entrance from a Ninja Duck changed everything. The silent figure ripped through the air and cast a brief shadow over the crowd. She swooped inches above their heads, ruffling the salon bleached tips of the Channel 12 camera man and dipping right in front of Camilla's microphone.

"Oooh," said the crowd, and "Aah!" as Duck pirouetted mid-air and came to land on the top of the fence next to Mrs. Flabbergast.

"You're early," she said in a whisper out of the side of her mouth. "We haven't done the sheep's chorus, or Hampton's race along the beach yet."

"There's been a change of plan," said Duck quietly. "Molly had a better idea. We've called in the Inspector."

"But Molly's at school."

"No, she's here with us. She couldn't leave us on a day like this. It's alright, she figured it all out. Trust me. Ah, fantastic, he's here at last."

"Who is here? Who are you talking about? Oh no, he's not supposed to be here for hours. He's far too early. We're not ready yet! We have to get the audience on our side first." Mrs. Flabbergast began to rub her hands together anxiously as she watched the garden gate open with a loud creak.

"Trust me," said Duck. "Or rather, trust Molly. She has a better plan - Mr. Bennet is going to help us save the farm. He just doesn't know it yet."

Mrs. Flabbergast wrinkled her nose. "Where is Molly then? How on earth could anyone get Mr. Bennet to help us? You must be joking, Duck, and this is not the time for jokes!"

Duck jumped up and spun in a complete circle and landed smoothly on the post again. The crowd oohed and aahed again at her skill. "Ladies and gentlemen," she called into the rabble, "let me introduce you to the most wonderful man, the most amazing inspector of farmyards you have ever had the pleasure to meet. He has never met a list he could not tick, a form he could not complete or a regulation he could not enforce."

As one, the crowd turned to see who Duck pointed at behind them. Mrs. Flabbergast frowned as she realized that Duck wasn't joking. An annoyed bowler hat wove its way through the huddle of reporters. Using a briefcase to drive a wedge in the tiniest of cracks and split it wide open, gradually the hat drew closer to the front.

Aha, thought Molly, *perfect timing.* She struggled up from the damp ground and stepped out from behind the chicken coop. Faking a confidence she did not feel, Molly took a deep breath and strode to the front of the pig pen.

"Mr. Bennet!" she called to the bowler hat. "How wonderful to see you. Do come and join us."

Other neighbors from further up the Crescent had followed him through the gate. Mr. and Mrs. Joseph from the end house tottered into view. Behind them Miss Thompson fluttered into the farmyard, still upset over the loss of her gnome and humorous fishing pole. Ravi and his whole family sidled in next and Molly watched as the small boy wriggled his way to the front of the pack, dragging his smallest sister with him, ahead of all the cameras and reporters.

It looked like everybody wanted to be at the farmyard to see the latest excitement. There were a lot of people in Chestnut Crescent who wanted to know the fate of their farm. The only people missing seemed to be the Henderson family.

Freya appeared from the shadows and crept along the rail to sit behind Molly.

"Did you tell them all to come?" asked Molly quietly. "No. Why do you think they're here?" Freya asked.

"I don't know. I thought they liked us. Or the eggs and the manure anyway. Was I wrong? I thought only the Hendersons had a problem with us. Is it everybody?"

Mr. Bennet reached the pig pen at last, red in the face and his hat askew. He did not look happy. In fact, he looked as unhappy as a talking pig in muck. He slammed his free hand down on the gate and sucked in a lungful of air, steadying himself after pushing through the crowd. "I knew it!" he said. "I knew something peculiar happened here."

Mrs. Flabbergast flapped nervously at him. "Of course you did, Mr. Bennet. Mr. Bennet here is very astute," she told the cameras and the thousands of watchers hanging onto her every word at the other end of the live television broadcast. "He has always known there is something very special about our little farm," she said. "We tried to keep it quiet, but he is right, the world should know about the amazing animals that live here."

"Amazing?" Mr. Bennet said, sputtering out the word and attempting to straighten his hat. "Amazing? Unconventional more like. Breaking all the rules and ignoring all the regulations. You'll be evicted today!" He slammed the briefcase onto the fence post and clicked the locks open. The cameras all zoomed in as out came the clipboard and clicky pen. "Under The Government Act of 1893 pertaining to the Inspection of Farmyard and Animal Husbandry Premises, I will be inspecting this farmyard immediately."

As if on cue, three heads popped up into view from the garden next door.

The Hendersons could almost have been expecting

this, thought Molly. *They were just waiting for Mr. Bennet to appear today*. She smiled sweetly at them. Petunia stuck her nose up in the air and sniffed loudly, while her parents glowered at Molly. Alastair was nowhere to be seen.

"Why?" asked Camilla Hughes, thrusting her microphone at Mr. Bennet. He grimaced and backed away rapidly from her. "What regulations are they breaking exactly Mr. Bennet? If they are talking animals, there could be a case for them to have human rights and then that would be a whole different set of rules, wouldn't it?"

CHAPTER TWENTY-FIVE

Mr. Bennet to the Rescue

"Talking animals?" said Mr. Bennet, thoroughly alarmed by the unexpected crowd. He had no idea what Camilla rattled on about.

"Yes. Talking animals. Surely you, as the Government Inspector for this farm, were aware that there were talking animals resident here?" Camilla beamed and fluffed her hair for the camera, and then dived right back in to attack the confused Mr. Bennet. "Or did you not know? Were you ignorant, Mr. Bennet?"

Mr. Bennet struggled with whether to admit to not knowing something or pretend that he had full control of the situation. He relished the thought of new rules to enforce. But then there were people breaking the rules. But maybe new forms to tick. Probably new regulations to uphold. ."There is no real proof that they are talking animals," he said, sputtering through his words. "They may sound like they are talking, and they may look like they are talking, but there have been no tests done, no lists checked, no boxes ticked. It is not conclusive. We must investigate immediately."

"Boo!" came a voice from above the fence. Mr. Henderson dangled half over the top of the wooden divide, waving an arm angrily at Mr. Bennet.

"Shame!" shouted Mrs. Henderson, perched on a step-stool to see from her garden. "They're breaking the rules."

The crowd, and the cameras, turned to the noisy next-door neighbors.

"Double check that list Mr. Bennet."

I know that's you, Mr. Henderson, thought Molly.

"Of course, you must follow procedure," said Molly. Everyone turned to her in surprise, including her grandmother.

"I don't know what you're all looking at. We do need to follow the rules, all of us. After all, this is a most unusual street," said Molly. "We're not even the most interesting house."

"Really?" said Mr. Bennet, smelling a rat of some shape, but not sure where it lurked and how it squeaked.

"We have the most unusual neighbors. Haven't you seen the architecture next door?" asked Freya, over Molly's shoulder. "It used to be just a plain old three-bedroom semi-detached house like most of the others. But now it is a wonderful example of how a few additions can make a small house so spacious." She purred with satisfaction at the nearest microphone.

"Additions?" Mr. Bennet's nose twitched in excitement, oblivious to the fact he had been addressed by a cat. The thought of broken regulations made his mustache bristle with excitement. He held up his clipboard and clicked his pen with excitement, poised to tick or cross whatever came his way.

"Well, there have been a few tweaks." Molly helpfully pointed out everything she described. "The solar panels do look a little odd, but of course it's all for the environment. I do think that four satellite dishes on one house might be a bit ugly." *I can list every single addition to the neighbors' house if that makes you happy.*

"Four?" Mr. Bennet squeaked. He clicked his pen several times. His mustache visibly shook.

"Oh yes. I'm sure it must all be above board though. The Hendersons are always so proper about everyone following all the neighborhood rules. I can't imagine that they would have done anything to break them," Molly said, trying to keep a straight face.

The cameras swung from Molly to a quieter Mr. Henderson, over to Mr. Bennet and across to an increasingly anxious Mr. Henderson. Camilla Hughes licked her lips wolfishly and stood ready to pounce with her microphone at whoever broke first.

Molly tensed as she watched the change in Mr. Bennet. His mouth clenched in a firm line but turned up at the ends in a tight smile. His eyes glowed like a man possessed. But then the excitement of the moment crashed straight into the core of sheer government official-ness and bounced away. The glow in his eyes faded and his mouth straightened.

"Nevertheless," he said.

We're finished. Done for.

A new voice piped up from the huddle of neighbors.

"Green tongue," it said.

Confusion buzzed through the crowd. They began to edge away from the mysterious stranger and a space formed around him. Molly squinted at the shadowy figure, but all she could see was a floppy straw sun hat and a big, flapping raincoat. Somewhere under the sun hat she caught a flash of dark glasses. It was all tied together with a trailing blue woolen scarf. Odd as it looked, Molly knew there was something familiar about the strange character.

"Ask them about the green tongues," he insisted. "And the spots. And the insane itching."

The neighbors chuckled loudly at the memory of the Hendersons running down the street, covered in spots and sticking out green tongues. Molly nodded and turned back to Mr. Bennet.

"Tongues? Spots? Itching? What are you talking about, young man... lady?... Erm" said Mr. Bennet.

"But surely," said Molly, "you must have heard about the Mystery Outbreak at number 14." Mr. Bennet had not heard though. He frowned as Molly pushed on.

"I'm sure that they would have informed the Environmental Health Agency. Didn't they? Oh yes, green tongues. Spots all over their faces. A strange itching all over. It was terrible. We're hoping it's not contagious, because if the animals catch it...." She let her words tail off into the silence.

Camilla Hughes inserted herself into the pause. "Exactly how valuable are these talking animals, Mrs. Flabbergast?" she demanded. "Our viewers want to know." Mr. Bennet's eyes glazed joyfully over as he thought of the paperwork this would all generate.

"Oh yes, the green tongues, the itching, the spots," went on Molly, "They ran screaming down the road with the horror of it all."

"Is this true Mr. Henderson?" asked Mr. Bennet, turning to the row of heads. "Did you have a Mysterious Outbreak of an unknown disease at your address?"

"A few days ago," added Molly, nodding sympathetically at the row of embarrassed faces next door. "We felt so awful for you, Mr. Henderson."

"It was them!" shouted Mr. Henderson at last. "Their fault. They did something to us to make us ill." He pointed desperately at Rosemary and Lavender. "It was the Common Lurgy!"

The pigs were mortified at the thought.

"Common? Us?" they muttered angrily to each other.

"Oh come now, Mr. Henderson," joined in Mrs. Flabbergast, "how on earth do you think we could have given you green tongues? That's a silly idea."

"But you did. You and your animals. It's a conspiracy. You made us ill. Too ill to play tennis even." He slapped the fence with his hand as the neighbors laughed openly now.

"Ooh, he did look funny jumping about trying to scratch hisself, didn't he Norman?" said Mrs. Joseph to her husband. The television cameras swung round to capture the sight of a 'local resident commenting on the situation'. Mrs. Joseph saw them turn towards her, folded her arms firmly in front of her and nodded. "It were ever so funny, but we didn't want to catch it did we Norman?"

Mr. Joseph merely grunted in agreement with his wife and kept his eyes firmly fixed on the possibly contagious neighbors hanging over the fence.

"I said to Norman, didn't I Norman, that it's not right that they can have nasty diseases right on our doorstep and not do nowt about them. You should do summat about it Mr. Bennet, you really should." Mrs. Joseph wagged a finger indignantly at Mr. Bennet.

"Should I take that as a complaint requiring investigation, madam?" asked Mr. Bennet, whipping out a fresh notebook from his suit pocket and brandishing the clicky pen to great effect.

"Aye," said Mr. Joseph, nodding wisely at Mr. Bennet.

"Aye, you should." Mrs. Joseph barely paused

before starting on her list of complaints. "And while you're at it lad, you should take a look at their ghosts. Yes, ghosts," she waggled a finger. "You lot. They have..." and at this point her eyes opened wide and her fingers splayed and clenched into claws, "ghosts!" Content to have added as much drama as possible to the situation, Mrs. Joseph smirked and folded her arms firmly back over her chest.

"Ghosts?" said Mr. Bennet. "As in..."

"Ghosts," agreed the mysterious stranger. "And ghoulies." He nodded, as if this settled the matter.

But Mr. Bennet was still perplexed by this turn in the conversation. He prodded it again. "Ghoulies?"

"Yeah. They're not wrong. That lot had us all up the other night with screaming and bright lights and yelling and all sorts. They said the house was haunted." Another neighbor had decided to join the adventure. Bob from number 5 was there to get revenge for his condemned yellow roses. "And how come they get away with adding extra sheds and building bedrooms and all that when I can't even keep my roses?"

Awash in a sea of roses and ghosts and green tongues, Mr. Bennet reached out for something familiar.

"You say they've been building extra bedrooms? I was not aware of building permits for extensions to buildings in this particular street. I presume you do have the required permits and council planning permissions and have requested the correct inspections pre- and post-work completion."

"I will need to see all that paperwork immediately, followed by a full inspection of the residence. I am calling in an emergency Health Department Inspection Team to go over number 14 with a fine-tooth comb to look for contagious outbreaks and diseases. I will be conferring with the local vicar about the possibility of supernatural activity at that residence. That address will need to be evacuated immediately. And, most importantly, I will be investigating the paper trail of permits and permissions for all the changes to the residence. I appreciate everyone's assistance in this matter."

In the brief silence, everyone tried to work out what Mr. Bennet had meant. Molly figured it out first and she looked up hopefully at the bowler-hatted hero.

"What does that mean for the Flabbergast Farm?" she asked. Everybody stared at Mr. Bennet, busily ticking and crossing away with his clicky pen, as happy as a donkey with a new straw hat.

Molly glanced over at her grandmother to see what she thought. Mrs. Flabbergast leaned back against the fencepost of the pigpen, one hand on hip and the other covering her mouth as she tried to smother her laughter. Her shoulders shook as she looked between the Henderson family and the happy Mr. Bennet. *That's got to be a good sign.*

"Mr. Bennet?" she said. "What will happen to the Farm?"

"Why nothing, of course." He barely looked up at her. "I was obligated to investigate the Flabbergast Farm because of complaints by some neighbors. However, since those neighbors themselves are now under investigation, their complaints are currently frozen." He looked around at the silent crowd. "Unless any other neighbors would like to make a complaint," he suggested, with a note of optimism in his voice.

A murmur of no's and of course not's rose up around him.

"Why would we do that?" asked Mrs. Joseph, beaming at the excitement she had caused. "We love having the farmyard here at the end of the street. How else would we get fresh eggs for breakfast and steaming compost for the gardens?"

"My party can go ahead?" asked Ravi, his face lighting up with a huge grin. "Excellent!"

Mr. Bennet's mustache twitched of its own accord. "Well if that's all ladies and gentlemen..."

Whoa. Hang on a minute...

"Wait. You mean there is no inspection for us today?"

"No, no inspection."

"You won't take Grandma's license?"

Is he for real?

"We can stay?"

Mr. Bennet clicked his clicky pen and put it in his jacket pocket. The clipboard went into the smart leather briefcase and he clicked the latches shut. Then he did a most unexpected thing. He winked an unmistakable wink at Mrs. Flabbergast, turned on his heel and marched from the farmyard without another word.

As if on a signal, a huge cheer went up from the crowd of neighbors and television crew and reporters and the animals joined in, honking and neighing and barking and clucking.

Only one person did not join in. One person remained stuck on the real reason they had come to the farm in the first place.

"But what about the talking goat and the talking llama?" said Camilla Hughes, her microphone still thrust out in front of her. Camilla wasn't always the fastest thinker, but once she had hold of an idea she was reluctant to let it go. "We need to hear from the goat and the llama and, I think, a cat," she persisted.

Molly froze at the sound of her voice. *How on earth will we get out of this one?* she wondered. *They've all heard Jinks and Larry and Freya talk, they're not going to forget that.* But Mrs. Joseph jumped in to save the day yet again.

"Oh, don't be ridiculous woman," she said. "Who'se goin' to believe that those animals talked really? Just a clever trick to get you all here and see that justice happened. Don't be so silly." She clapped Camilla across the back with enthusiasm, and Camilla pitched forward into a well-placed puddle of mud. Molly and her grandma looked at each other and grinned. *Sometimes, getting to know your neighbors can be so rewarding.*

"Would anyone like a nice cup of tea and some leek and pineapple tart before we have to start mucking out the animals?" asked Mrs. Flabbergast over the sea of voices. The crowd answered her with another cheer. She wrapped an arm around Molly's shoulders and pulled her in close for a hug. "I knew you'd come up with something to save us," she said.

Molly looked for the mysterious stranger in the crowd who had helped her to do just that. But he had disappeared. *I'll have to thank him later,* thought Molly.

CHAPTER TWENTY-SIX

And That was Nearly the End of That...

There were no reports of talking animals on the television that day, and no reports of unusual farm behavior in the local newspapers. Even Mr. Henderson knew better than to let that cat out of the bag.

The following morning, Alastair sneaked into the farmyard through the sliding fence panel.

Molly was collecting eggs inside the coop when she heard the tell-tale creak.

"Is that your new friend, Molly?" asked Bella, settling herself back down on her nest. "That boy from next door. Are you sure we can trust him?"

"Oh, I think he's a bit different from the rest of his family," said Molly. "If you give him a chance, he might surprise you." She backed out of the chicken coop and trotted over to Alastair. "Morning! How much trouble did you get into with your dad for helping us yesterday?"

"I have absolutely no idea what you're talking about," said Alastair, with a twinkle in his eye. "I was upstairs, sitting quietly in my bedroom when you were making all that fuss over here with the TV people. I only found out about it when Petunia came in yelling about talking goats. Very strange."

"Of course," said Molly, playing along, "You weren't over here sporting a big floppy sun hat and shouting out helpful comments at all." She smiled shyly at him. "We're all grateful you know. I was beginning to run out of ideas."

"I don't know what you mean." He grinned at her. "You just needed to be reminded about what you'd already done, that's all. Those tricks were really clever."

"Don't you mind that your dad's in trouble?"

"Nah. He's brought it all on himself, and he might have got away with it if he hadn't tried to get you lot kicked out. Besides, it's going to cost him an awful lot of money to set it all right, so it looks as if we won't be able to be members of the Tennis Club for a while. I can't tell you how happy I am about that!" He laughed at her expression. "Hey, cheer up, I might even have to start going to your school now too. Even Mum realizes we probably can't afford fancy private school right now, so we might actually get to go to a normal one. It sounds like a right laugh."

Molly wasn't sure what stories he'd been hearing

about her school, but as long as he was happy, it wasn't important.

It became a lot quieter and much friendlier in Chestnut Crescent over the next few weeks. Everything settled down and life went back to what passed as normal at the Flabbergast Farm.

Yellow rose bushes bloomed along the front gardens. Several front doors were repainted a bright shiny red overnight. The neighborhood kids started coming to help muck out on a Saturday morning. Donald gave them donkey rides up and down the Crescent as a reward. Ravi's party was a huge success, and Jinx ate so much cake that he made himself sick.

Bella laid two brown eggs and Robbie the Rooster went round the whole farmyard telling everyone about it. Donald got a new sunflower for his straw hat. This one was extra-large and a bright yellow. Rosemary and Lavender were given a new game of scrabble since theirs had lost so many pieces during Mr. Bennet's inspection.

Mrs. Joseph continued to pop over several afternoons a week for a friendly cup of tea and a slice of unusual cake. Molly often saw her stopping for a chat with Jinks as she left, clutching a tray full of fresh eggs.

Printed in Great Britain
by Amazon

36883668R00116